THE RACONTEURS
CONSOLERS OF THE LONELY

GW00660637

PUBLISHED BY
WISE PUBLICATIONS
14-15 BERNERS STREET, LONDON, W1T 3LJ, UK.

EXCLUSIVE DISTRIBUTORS:
MUSIC SALES LIMITED
DISTRIBUTION CENTRE, NEWMARKET ROAD,
BURY ST EDMUNDS, SUFFOLK, IP33 3YB, UK.

MUSIC SALES PTY LIMITED
20 RESOLUTION DRIVE, CARINGBAH,
NSW 2229, AUSTRALIA.

ORDER NO. AM994906
ISBN 978-1-84772-672-8

THIS BOOK © COPYRIGHT 2008 WISE PUBLICATIONS,
A DIVISION OF MUSIC SALES LIMITED.

EDITED BY TOM FARNCOMBE.
MUSIC ARRANGED BY MARTIN SHELLARD.
MUSIC PROCESSED BY PAUL EWERS MUSIC DESIGN.

PRINTED IN THE EU.

WWW.MUSICSALES.COM

WISE PUBLICATIONS
part of The Music Sales Group
London/New York/Paris/Sydney/Copenhagen/Berlin/Madrid/Tokyo

CONSOLER OF THE LONELY

WORDS & MUSIC BY
JACK WHITE & BRENDAN BENSON

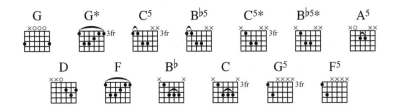

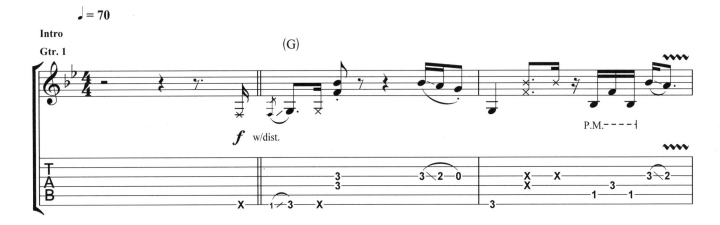

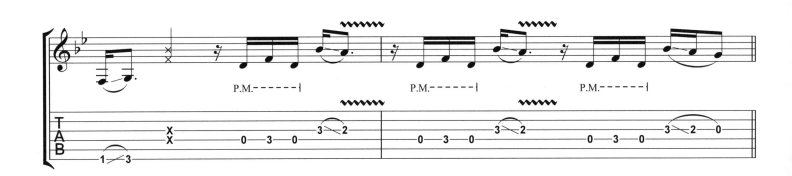

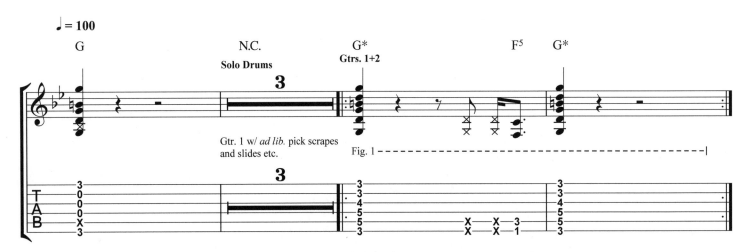

Verse G*

1. Have - n't seen the sun in weeks,_ my skin is get - ting pale._

Gtrs. 1+2 w/ Fig. 1

F⁵ G*

Have - n't got a mind left to speak and I'm skin - ny as a rail._

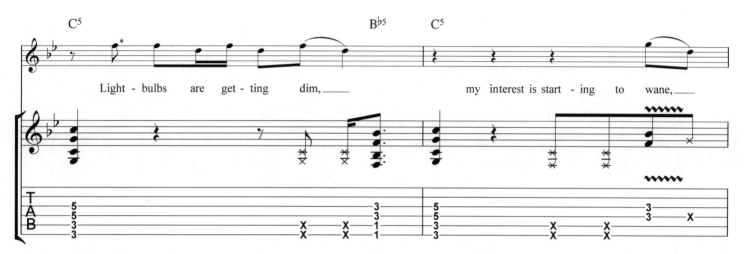

C⁵ B♭⁵ C⁵

Light - bulbs are get - ting dim,_ my interest is start - ing to wane,_

* Cont. vocal harmony sim. ad lib.

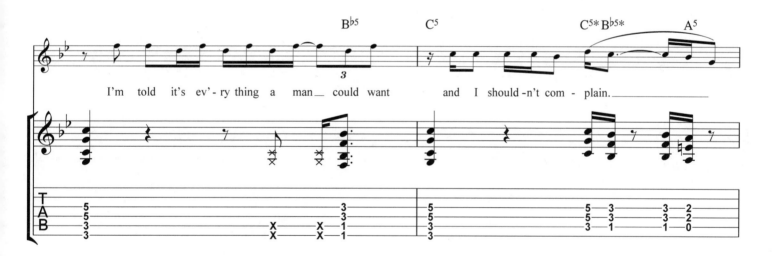

B♭⁵ C⁵ C⁵* B♭⁵* A⁵

I'm told it's ev' - ry thing a man_ could want and I should -n't com - plain._

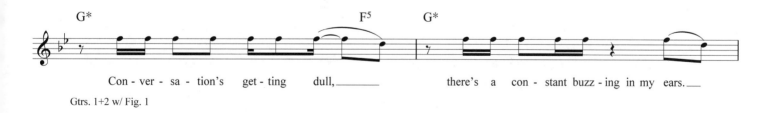

G* F⁵ G*

Con - ver - sa - tion's get - ting dull,_ there's a con - stant buzz - ing in my ears._

Gtrs. 1+2 w/ Fig. 1

F⁵ G*

Sense of hu - mour's void_ and null and I'm bored to tears.

4

Ah,_____ look - ing for sym - pa - thy.

I can get you some - thing, a - some - thing good,_ a - some - thing good to eat.

♩ = 100

Verse

2. Have - n't had a de - cent meal, my brain is fried. Have - n't slept a wink for real,_____

my tongue is tied._____ Light bulbs are get - ting dim,_ my in - terest is start - ing to wane,

I'm told it's ev' - ry - thing a man_ could want and I should - n't com - plain._____

5

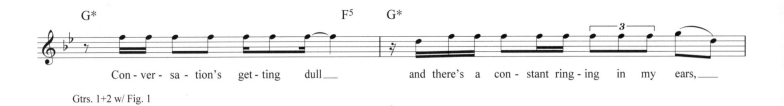

Con - ver - sa - tion's get - ting dull___ and there's a con - stant ring - ing in my ears,___

Gtrs. 1+2 w/ Fig. 1

Sense of hu - mour's void___ and null and I'm bored to tears.

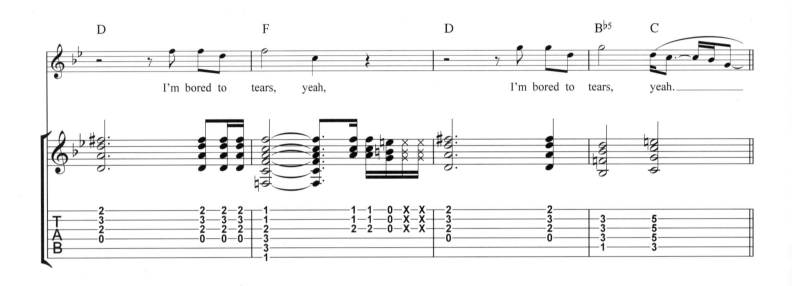

I'm bored to tears, yeah, I'm bored to tears, yeah.___

Double time

Interlude

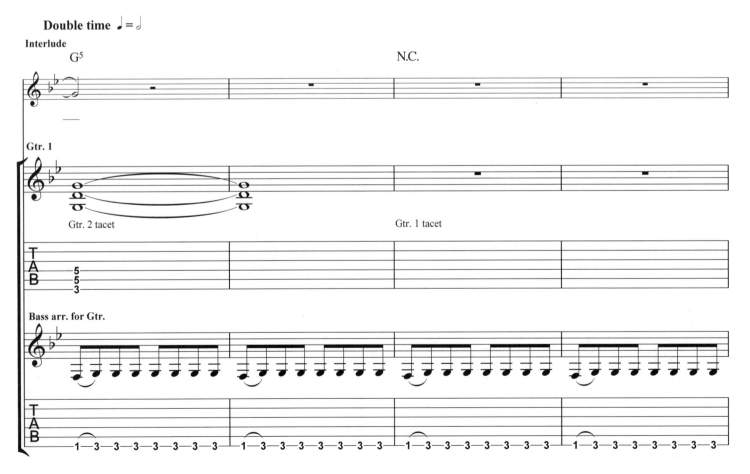

Gtr. 1

Gtr. 2 tacet   Gtr. 1 tacet

Bass arr. for Gtr.

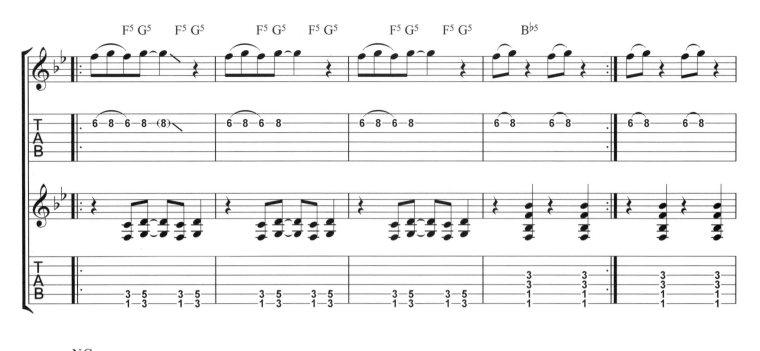

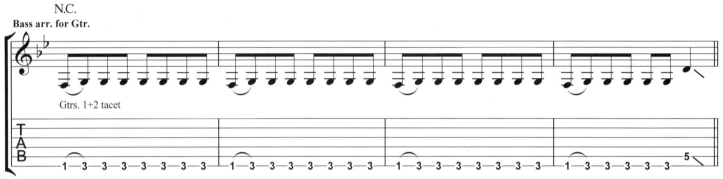

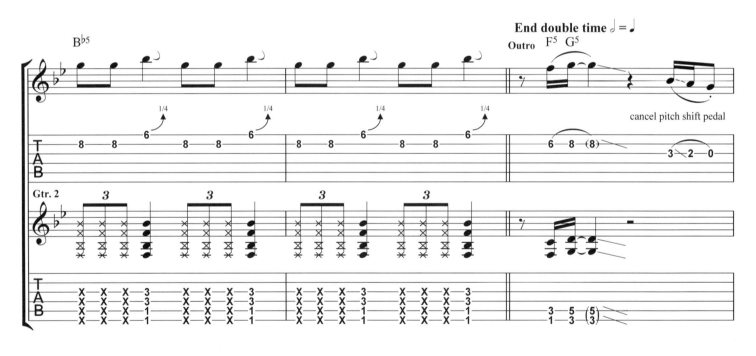

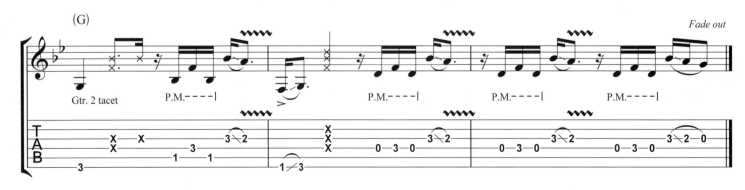

8

SALUTE YOUR SOLUTION

WORDS & MUSIC BY
JACK WHITE & BRENDAN BENSON

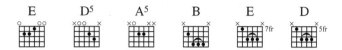

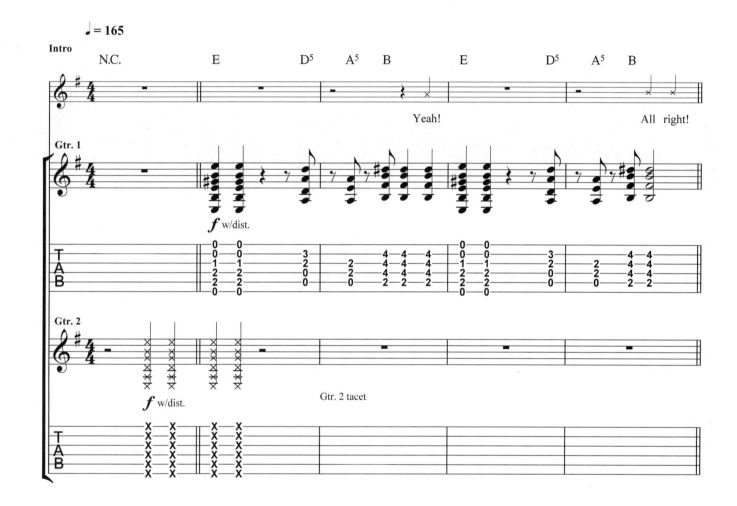

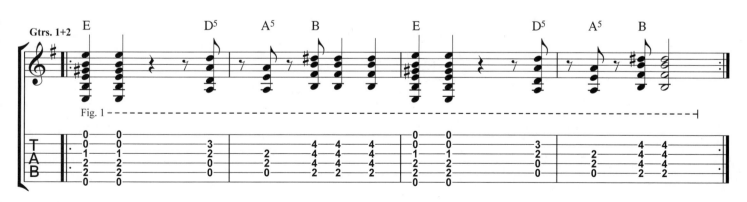

Verse

1. I seem to think, I think I've got a lit - tle si - tu - a - tion,
2. I find my - self just look - ing well be - yond my best in - ten - tions,

so lis - ten to me, sis - ter, lis - ten, may - be you can help. I think I give a lot of
ig - nor - ing an - y kind of prize I might re - ceive at all. While oth - ers seem to find the

Organ Solo

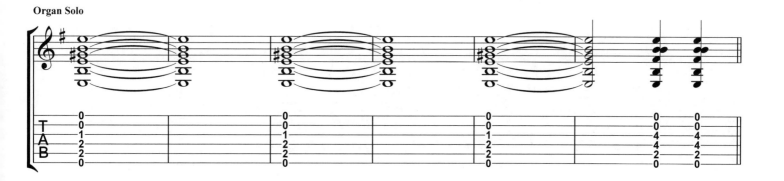

Bridge

Gtr. 1 (E)

w/fuzz

Gtr. 2 tacet

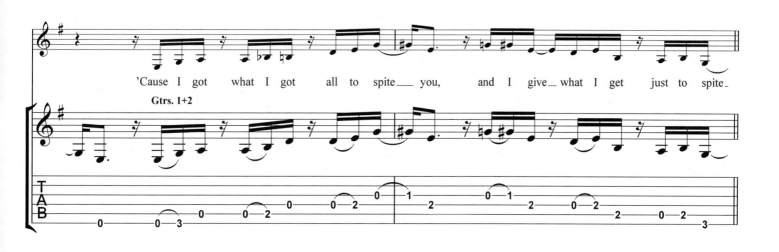

'Cause I got what I got all to spite___ you, and I give___ what I get just to spite___

Gtrs. 1+2

1.

___ you. And I got what I got all to spite___ you, and I give___ what I get just to spite

— you, and I give what I get just to spite___(you.)

Verse

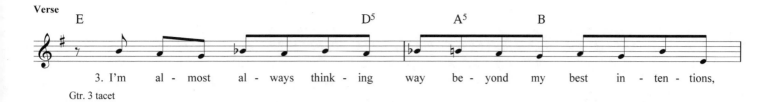

3. I'm al - most al - ways think - ing way be - yond my best in - ten - tions,

Gtr. 3 tacet

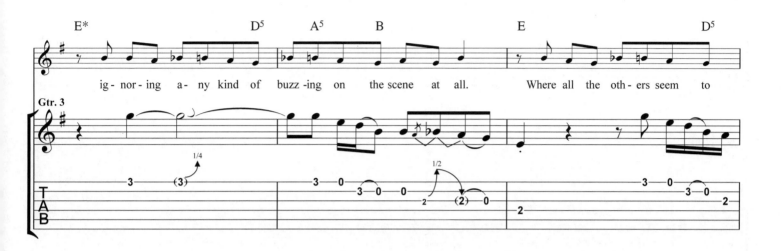

ig - nor - ing a - ny kind of buzz - ing on the scene at all. Where all the oth - ers seem to

Gtr. 3

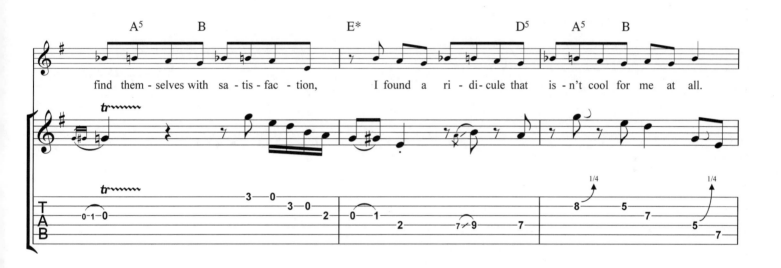

find them - selves with sa - tis - fac - tion, I found a ri - di - cule that is - n't cool for me at all.

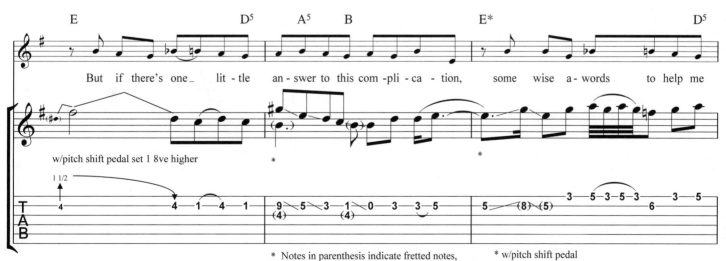

But if there's one_ lit - tle an - swer to this com - pli - ca - tion, some wise a - words to help me

w/pitch shift pedal set 1 8ve higher

* Notes in parenthesis indicate fretted notes, * w/pitch shift pedal
other pitches are produced by use of pitch shift pedal

YOU DON'T UNDERSTAND ME

WORDS & MUSIC BY
JACK WHITE & BRENDAN BENSON

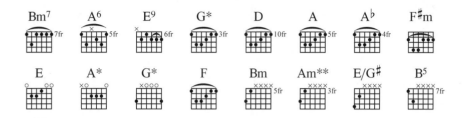

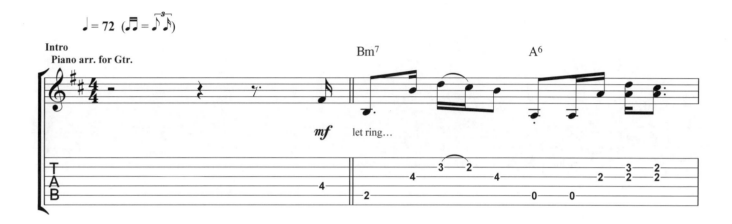

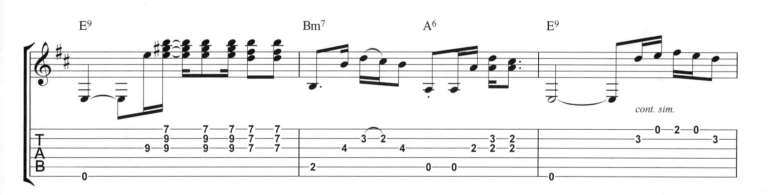

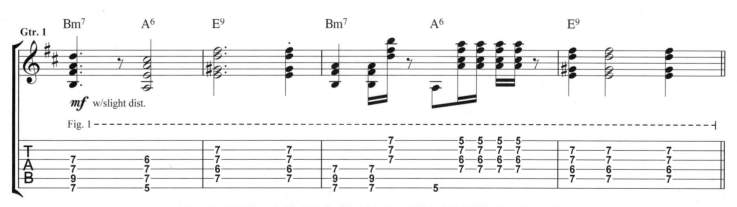

Verse

1. You don't un-der-stand_ me,_____ but if the feel-ing was right, you might

Gtr. 1 plays Fig. 1

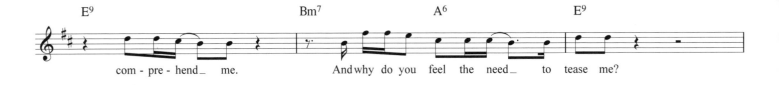

com-pre-hend_ me. And why do you feel the need_ to tease me?

Why don't you turn it a-round?_ It might be ea-si-er to please_ me. And there's al-

Chorus

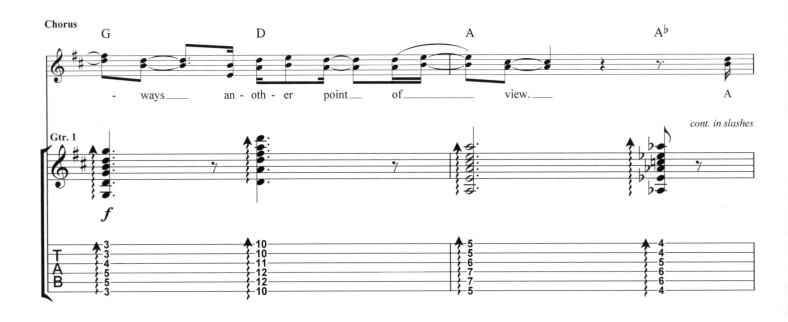

-ways_____ an-oth-er point_ of_____ view._____

A

cont. in slashes

Gtr. 1

f

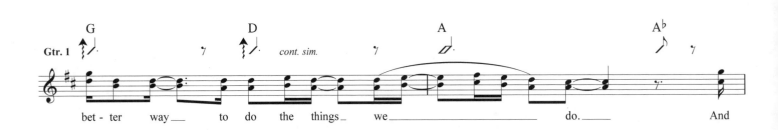

bet-ter way_____ to do the things_ we_____ do._____ And

18

how can you know me and I know you if no-thing is

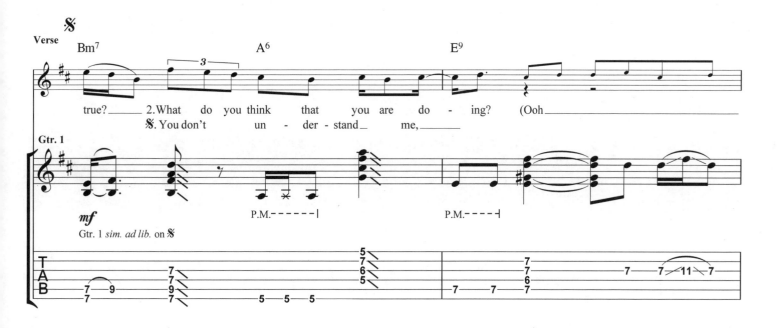

true? 2.What do you think that you are do - ing? (Ooh
You don't un - der - stand me,

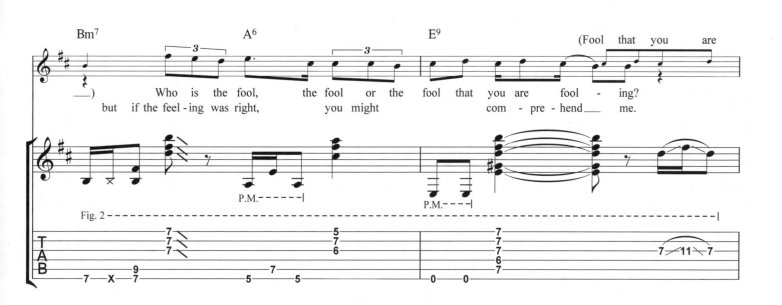

(Fool that you are
Who is the fool, the fool or the fool that you are fool - ing?
but if the feel - ing was right, you might com - pre - hend me.

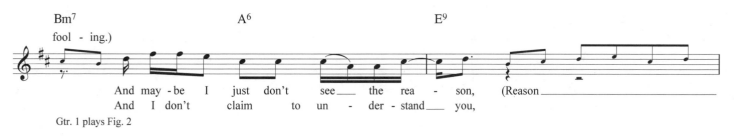

fool - ing.)
And may - be I just don't see the rea - son, (Reason
And I don't claim to un - der - stand you,

Gtr. 1 plays Fig. 2

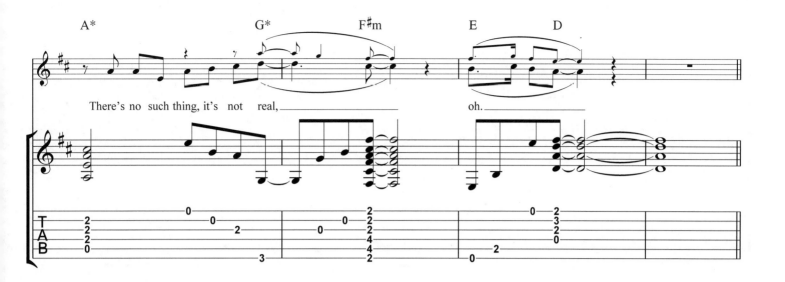

There's no such thing, it's not real,_____ oh._____

Interlude

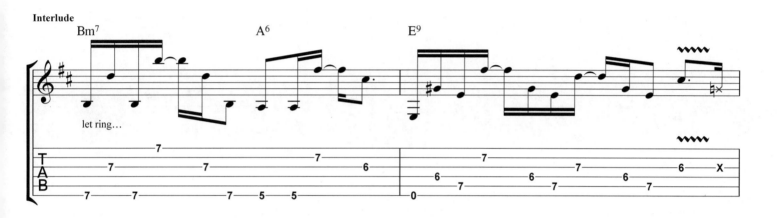

let ring…

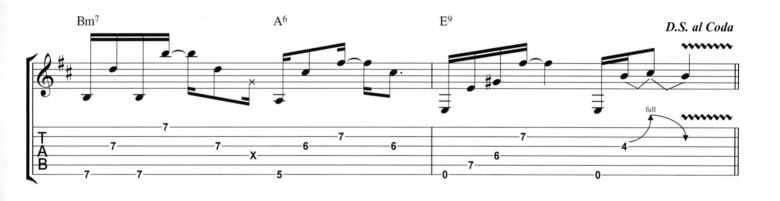

D.S. al Coda

𝄌 *Coda*

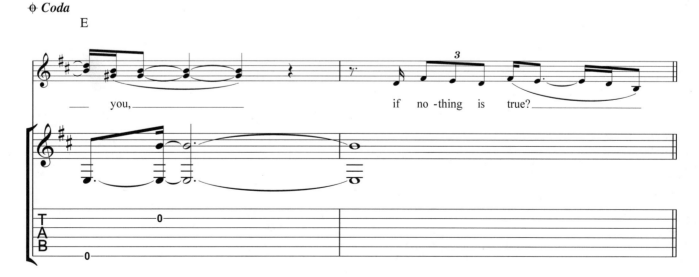

_____ you,_____ if no-thing is true?_____

OLD ENOUGH

WORDS & MUSIC BY
JACK WHITE & BRENDAN BENSON

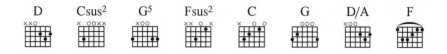

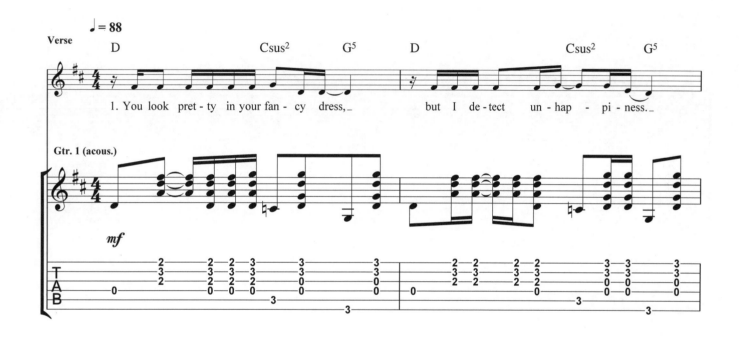

Verse

1. You look pret-ty in your fan-cy dress,_ but I de-tect un-hap-pi-ness._

Gtr. 1 (acous.)

You nev-er speak, so I have_ to guess,_ you're not free._

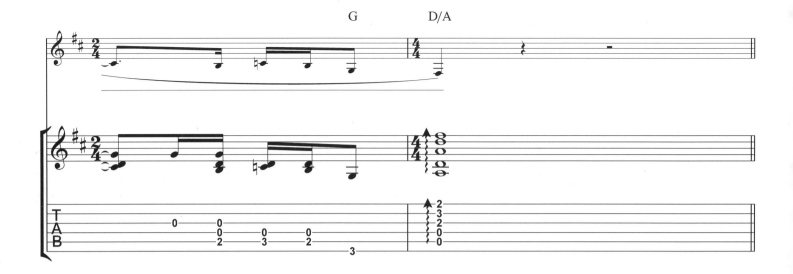

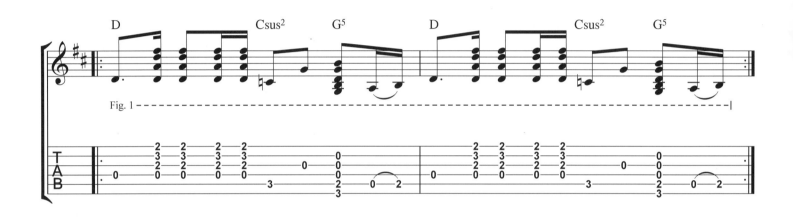

Verse

2. Yeah, may be when you're old e- nough, you'll re - al - ise that you're not___ so tough,___

3. You're too young to have it fi - gured out,___ you think you know what you're talk - ing a - bout.___

Gtr. 1 w/ Fig. 1

and some days the seas___ get rough and you'll see.___

you think it all will work___ it - self out but we'll see.___

Gtr. 1

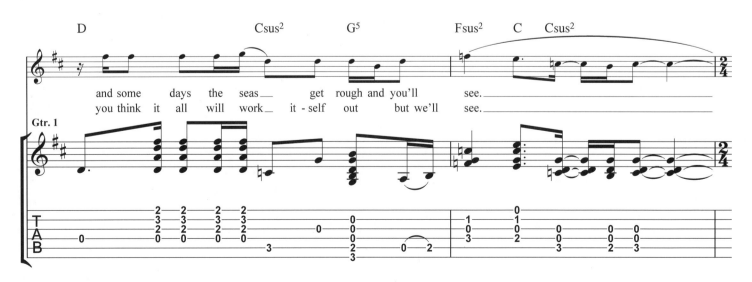

24

25

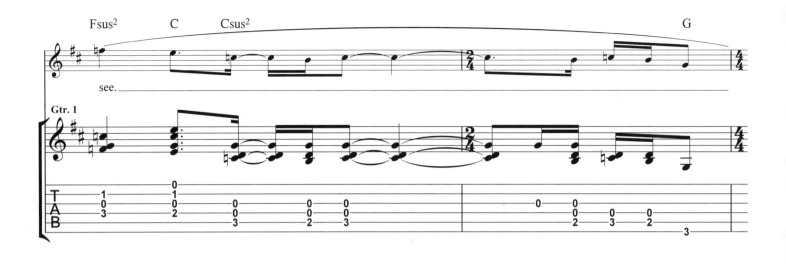

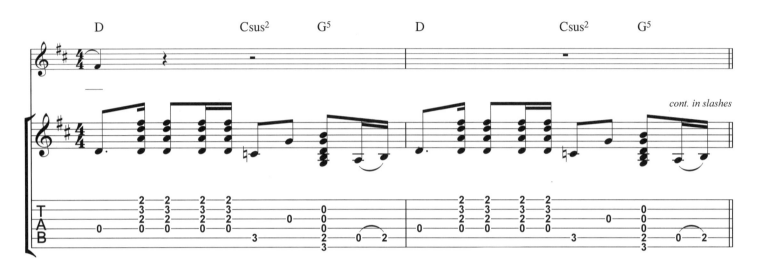

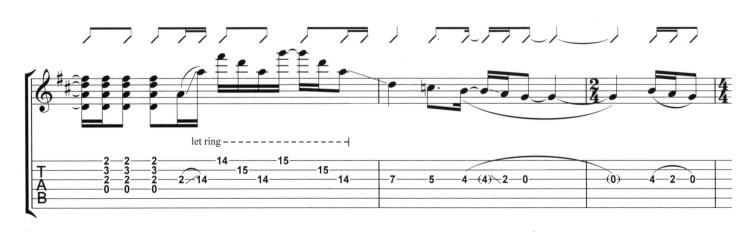

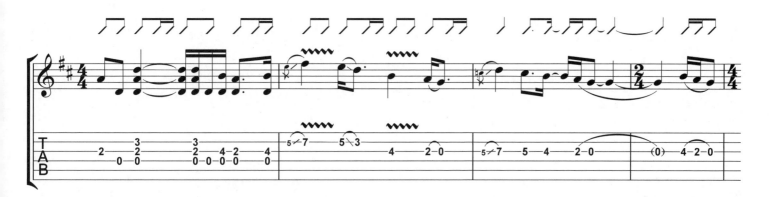

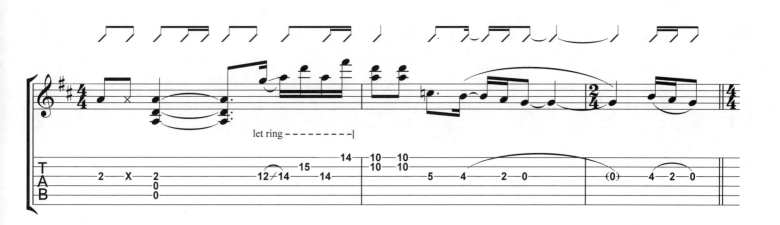

Bridge

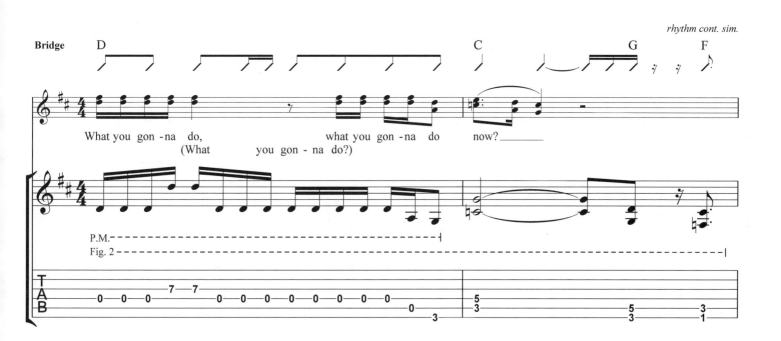

What you gon - na do, what you gon - na do now?
(What you gon - na do?)

What you gon - na do, what you gon - na do now?
(What you gon - na do?)

Gtr. 2 w/ Fig. 2

What you gon - na do, what you gon - na do now?
(What you gon - na do?)

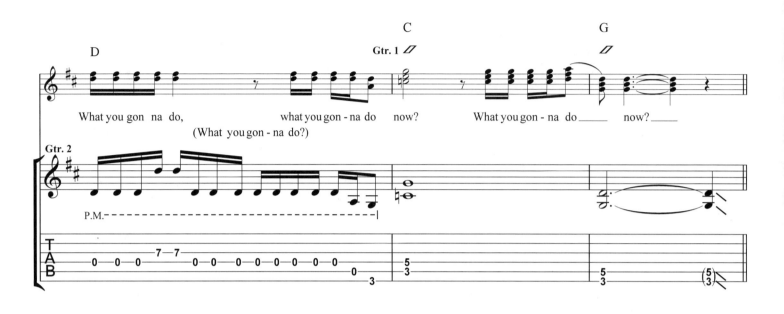

What you gon na do, what you gon - na do now? What you gon - na do_____ now?_____
(What you gon - na do?)

Gtr. 2

P.M.----------------------

Interlude

Gtrs. 4+5 (acous.)

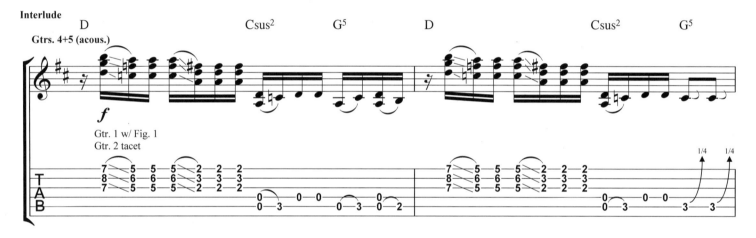

f

Gtr. 1 w/ Fig. 1
Gtr. 2 tacet

D.S. al Coda

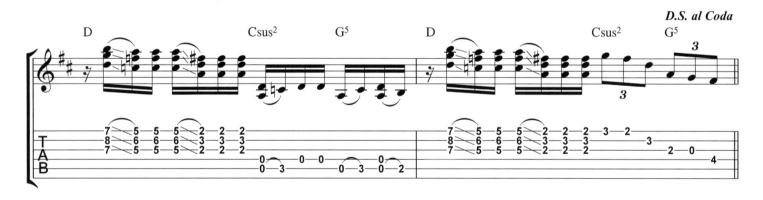

Coda

Yeah, ba - by, when you're old e - nough, ba - by, when you're old e - nough,

Gtr. 1 w/ Fig. 1

ba - by, when you're old   e - nough, you're not   free._____   yeah,__ you're not

Outro

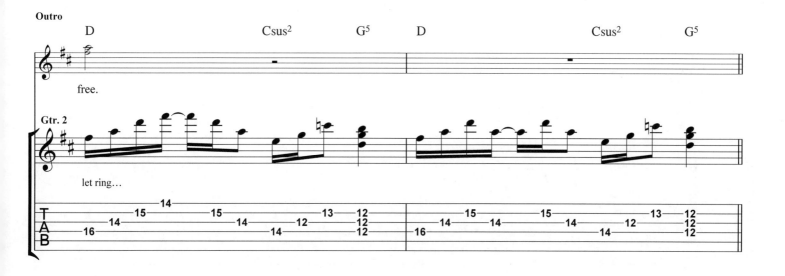

free.

Gtr. 2

let ring…

Play 3 times

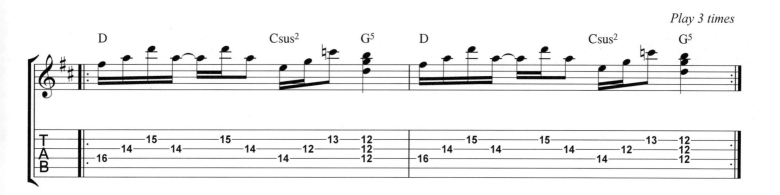

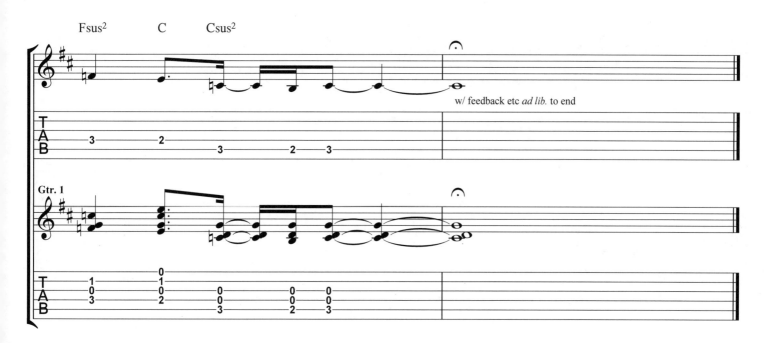

w/ feedback etc *ad lib.* to end

Gtr. 1

THE SWITCH AND THE SPUR

WORDS & MUSIC BY
JACK WHITE & BRENDAN BENSON

1. In the heat of the de - sert sun, ___ on the blist - er - ing trail,
2. The ri - der hal - lu - ci - nates, ___ the stamp - ing hooves on the sand.

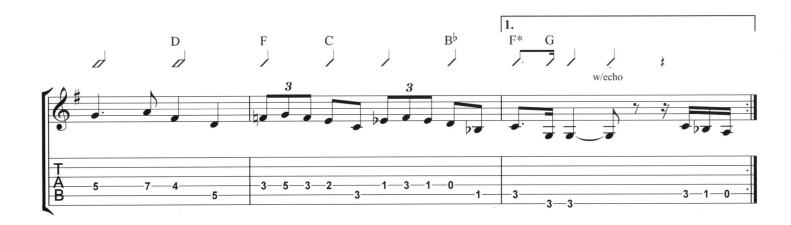

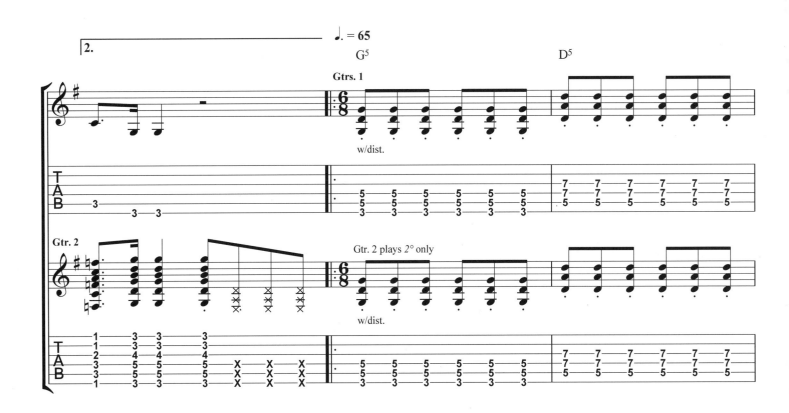

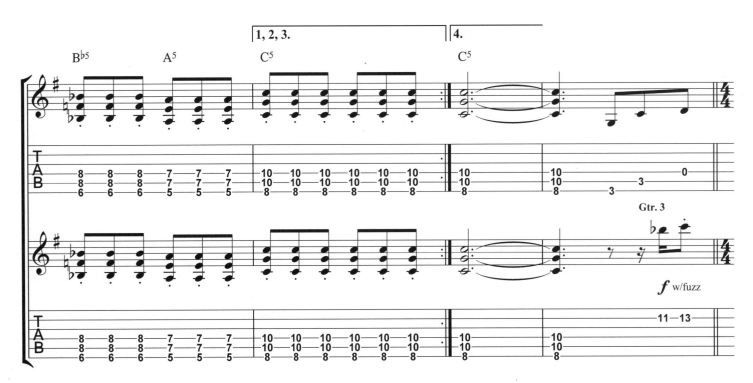

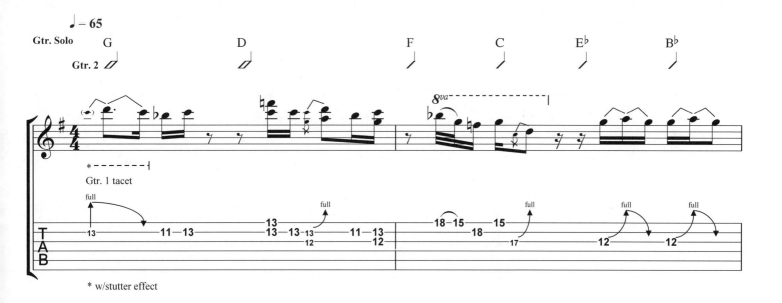

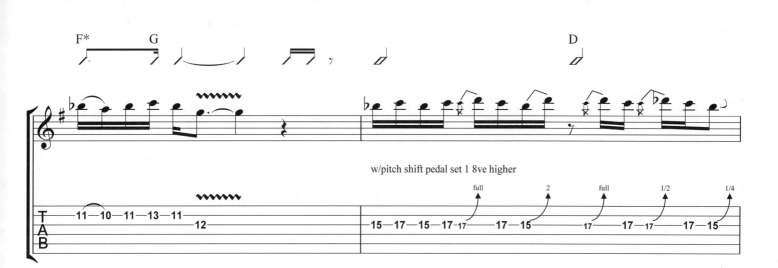

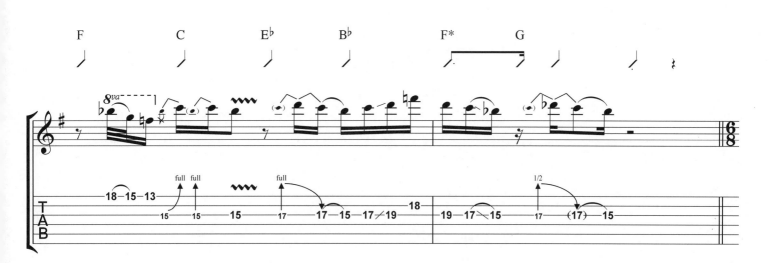

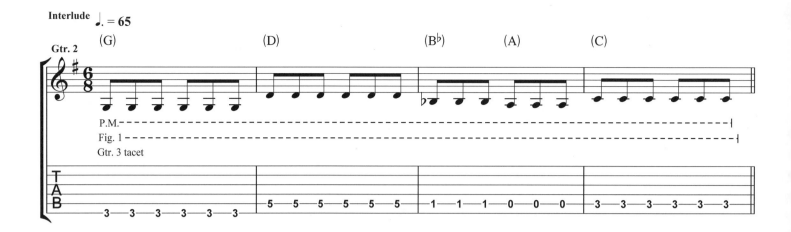

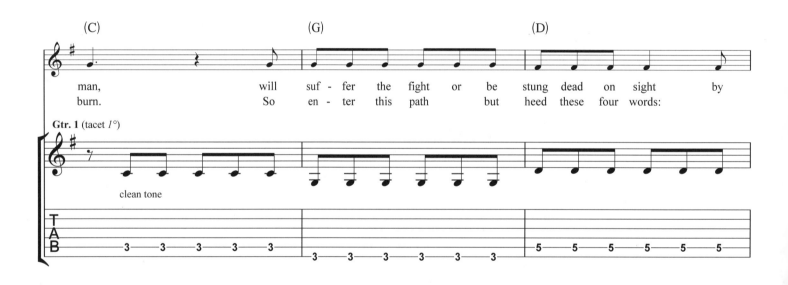

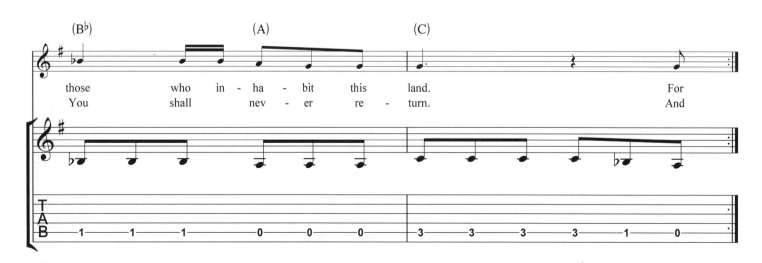

An - y poor souls who tres - pass a - gainst___ us,
theirs is the pow - er and this is their king - dom, as
Gtr. 1 w/ Fig. 2
Vocal doubled 8ve below *ad lib.*

wheth - er it be beast or man, will suf - fer the bite or be
sure as the sun does burn. So en - ter this path but

stung dead on sight by those who in - ha - bit this land. For
heed these four words: You shall nev - er re - turn.

Outro

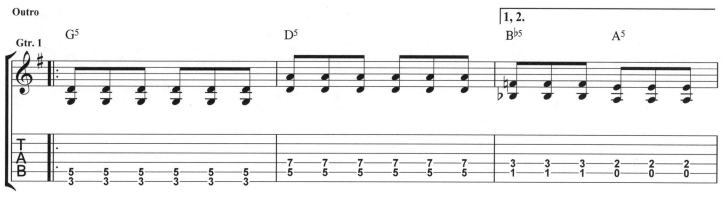

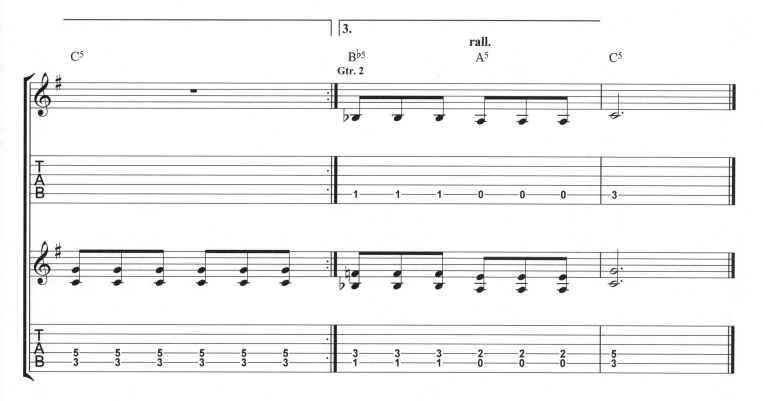

HOLD UP

WORDS & MUSIC BY
JACK WHITE & BRENDAN BENSON

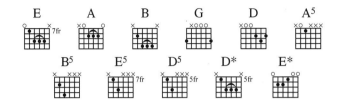

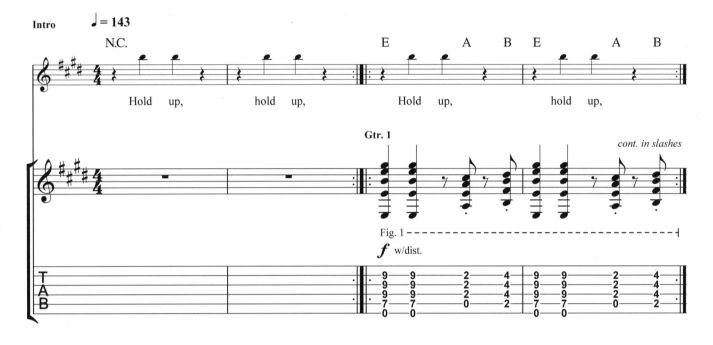

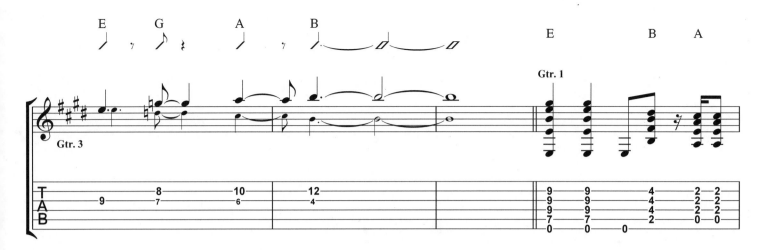

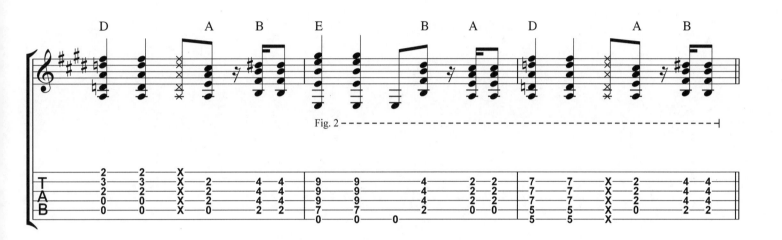

Verse

Gtr. 1 w/ Fig. 2

1. Had e-nough of these mod-ern times, a - bout to drive me out of my mind.
2. Friends took me to a freak show, but I think I've seen it all be-fore, well.
%. Modern girl you're so kind. you're gon-na help me get through this time.

And you know this too well, I'm holed up in my lit-tle cell, yeah!
Can I get a look at you, girl? May - be take a peek in your world, yeah!
And you know me too well, you didn't break a bone you broke in - to my prison cell.

Chorus

To Coda

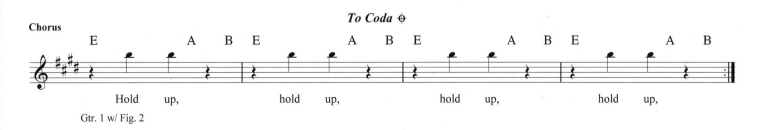

Gtr. 1 w/ Fig. 2

Hold up, hold up, hold up, hold up,

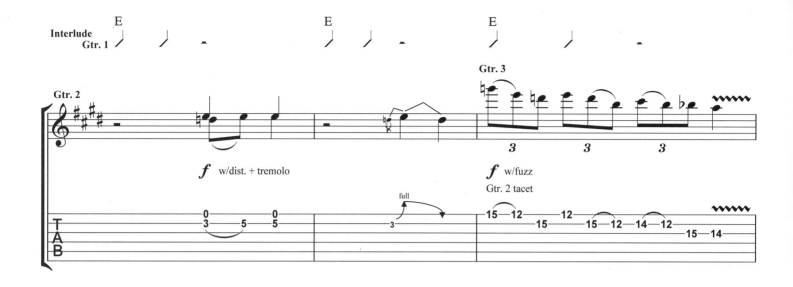

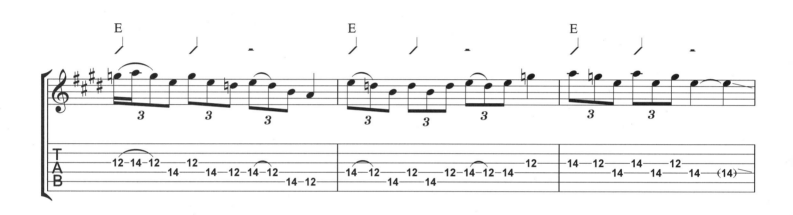

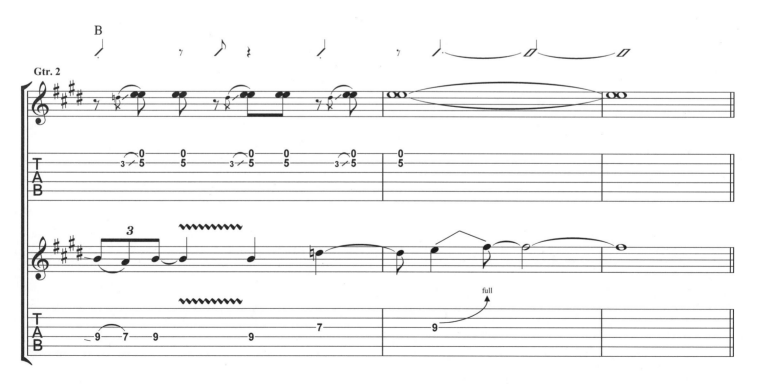

Interlude

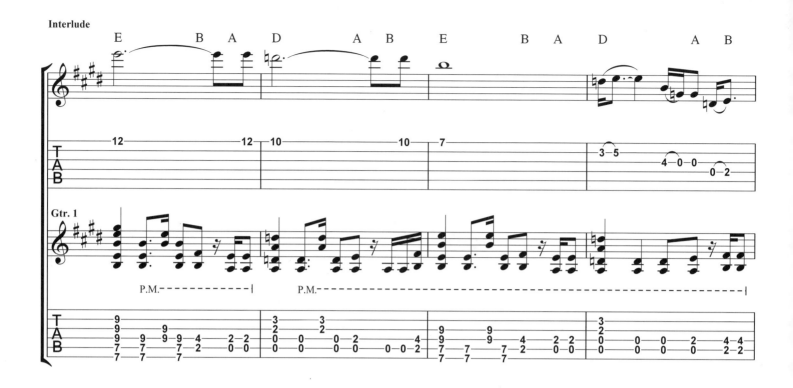

Organ Solo

D.S. al Coda

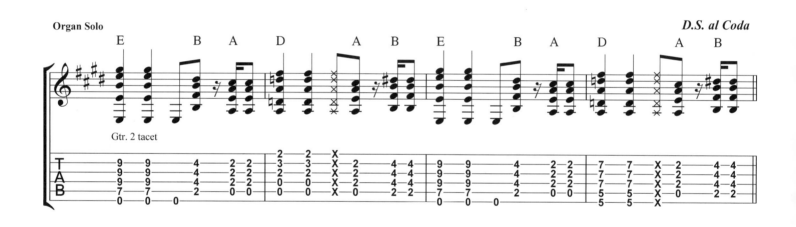

⊕ *Coda*

I'm holed up,   Hold up,

40

I'm holed up,

TOP YOURSELF

WORDS & MUSIC BY
JACK WHITE & BRENDAN BENSON

To match recording, tune all guitars slightly flat.

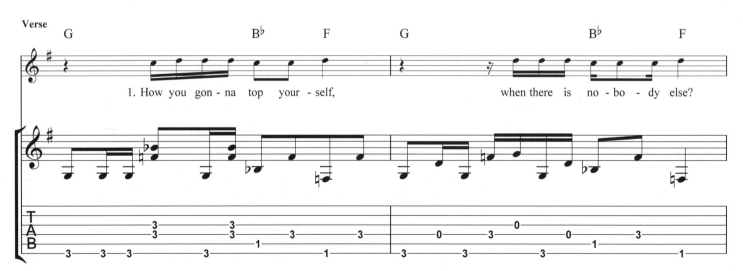

1. How you gon - na top your - self, when there is no - bo - dy else?

How you gon -na do it by your - self, 'cause I'm not gon -na be here to help__ you.__

Gtr. 2 (elec.)

w/slide
mf w/dist.

* tap on soundboard

Fig. 1

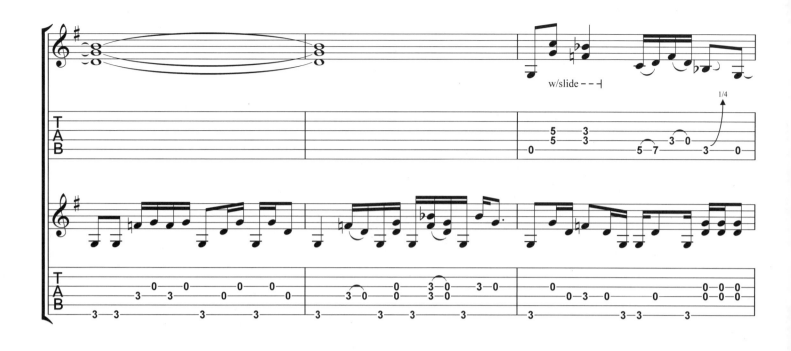

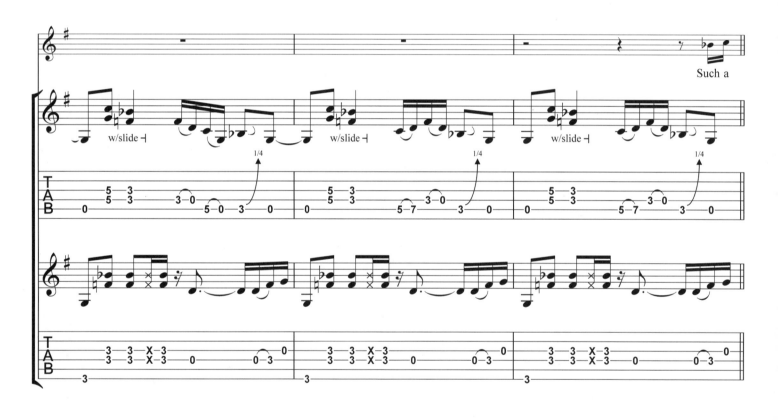

Such a

Bridge (G)

lit -tle girl, like a spin-ning top ma -ma, but she spin -ning out of con -trol. Yeah,

46

47

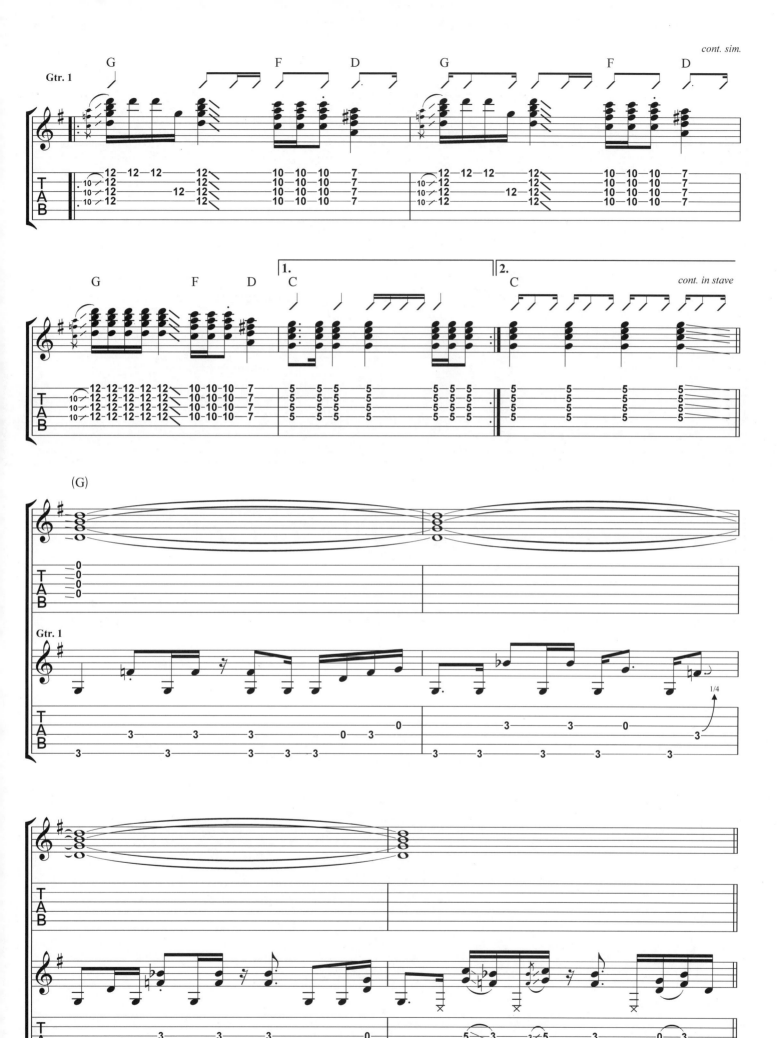

MANY SHADES OF BLACK

WORDS & MUSIC BY
JACK WHITE & BRENDAN BENSON

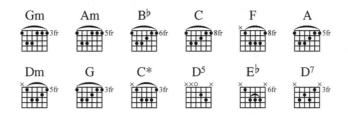

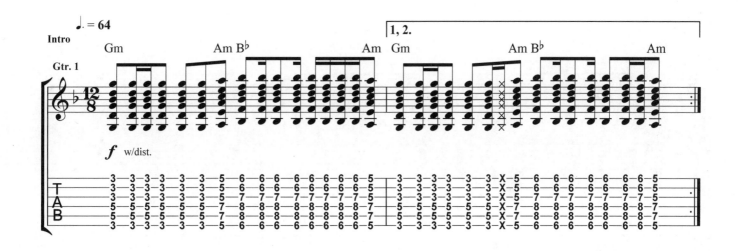

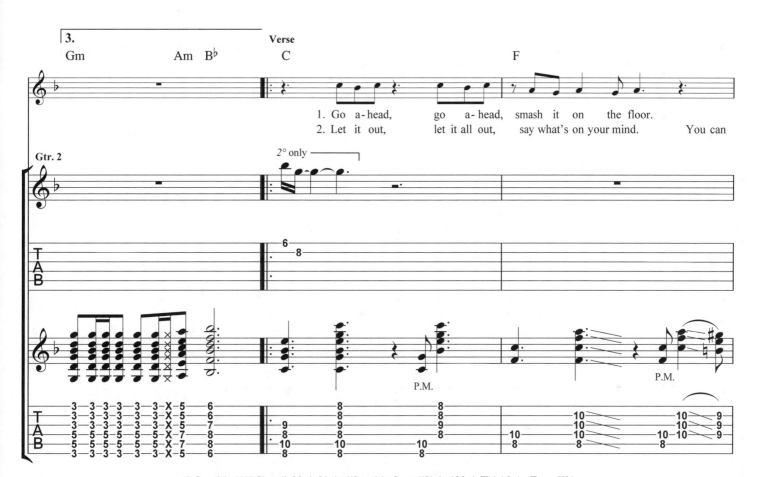

Ev -'ry-bo - dy sees___ and ev -'ry-one a - grees,___ that you and I___ are wrong,_ and it's

been that way __ too long. __ Take it as it comes_ and be thank-ful when it's done._ There's so

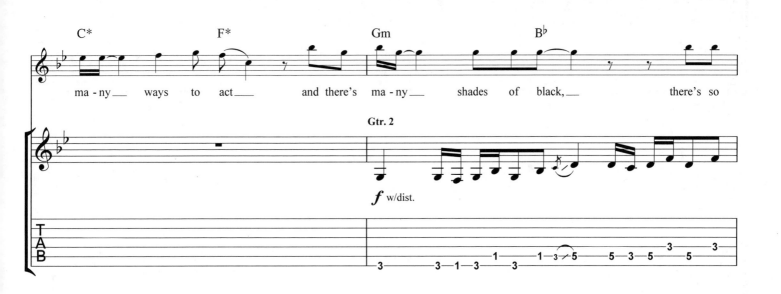

ma - ny___ ways to act___ and there's ma - ny___ shades of black,___ there's so

ma - ny___ shades of black,___ there's so ma - ny___ shades_ of black._

53

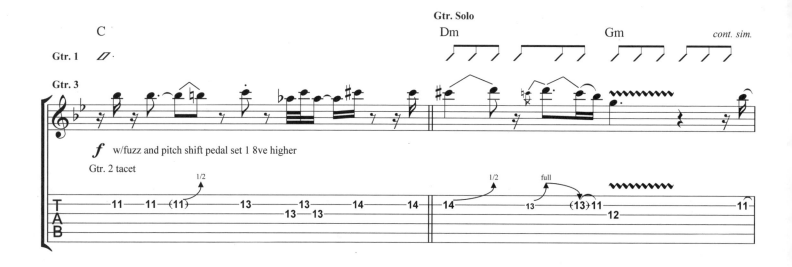

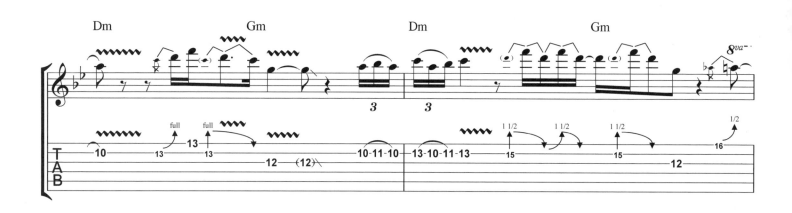

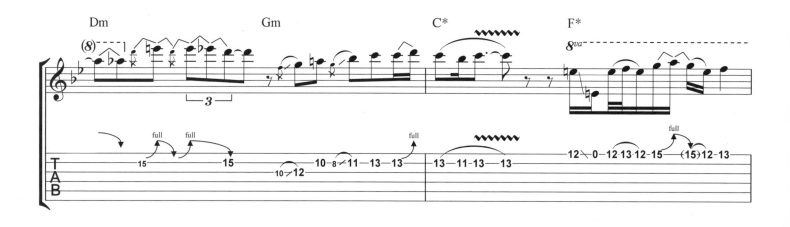

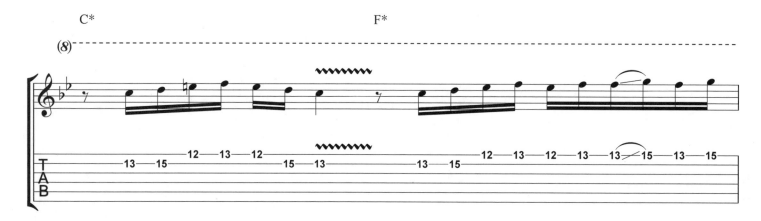

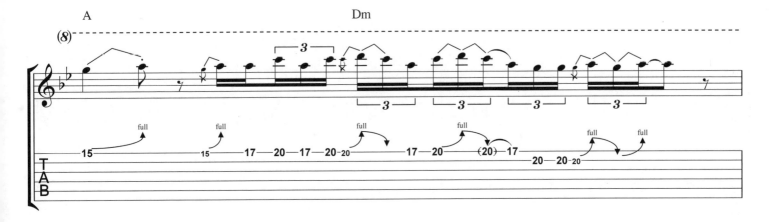

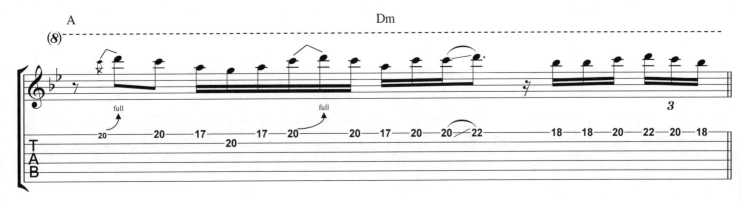

Ev - 'ry - bo - dy sees _____ and ev - 'ry - one a - grees, _____ that

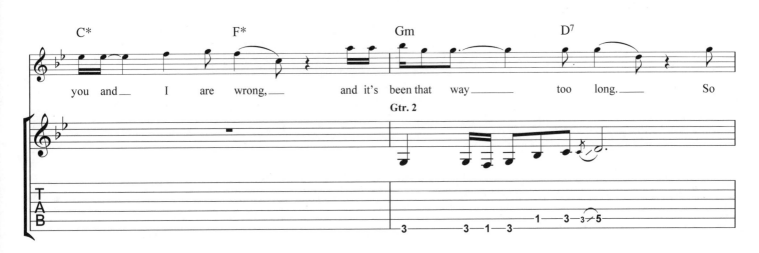

you and ___ I are wrong, ___ and it's been that way _____ too long. ___ So

56

FIVE ON THE FIVE

WORDS & MUSIC BY
JACK WHITE & BRENDAN BENSON

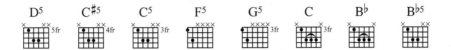

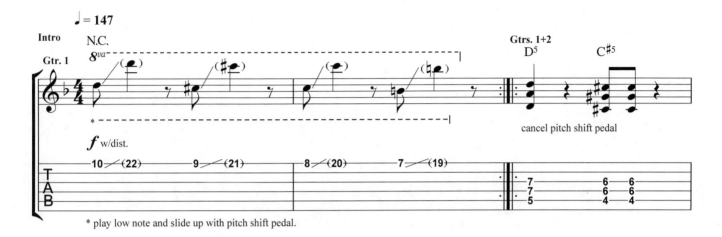

* play low note and slide up with pitch shift pedal.

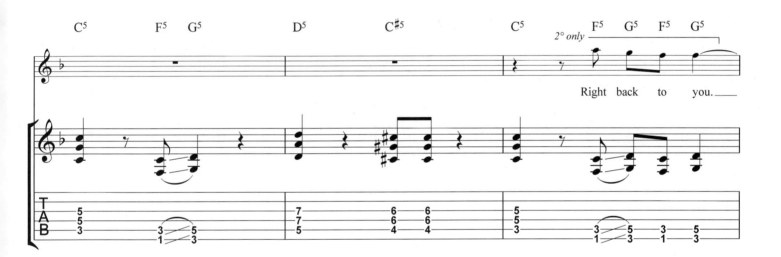

oh._____ If we keep it a - live, I'll ig - nore____ all the signs___ and keep driv -

-ing home,

right back to you.

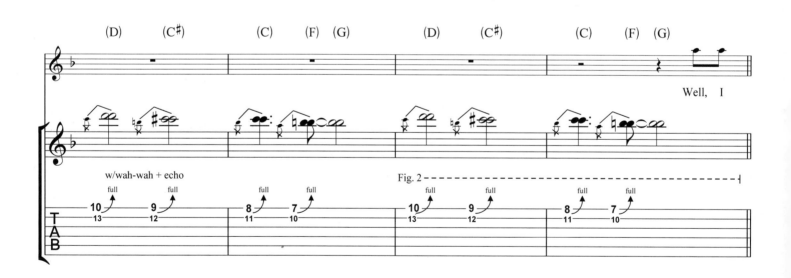

love you well e - nough, that I'll have you know.   The day I found you, girl, my life be - came ste -

Gtr. 2 w/ Fig. 2

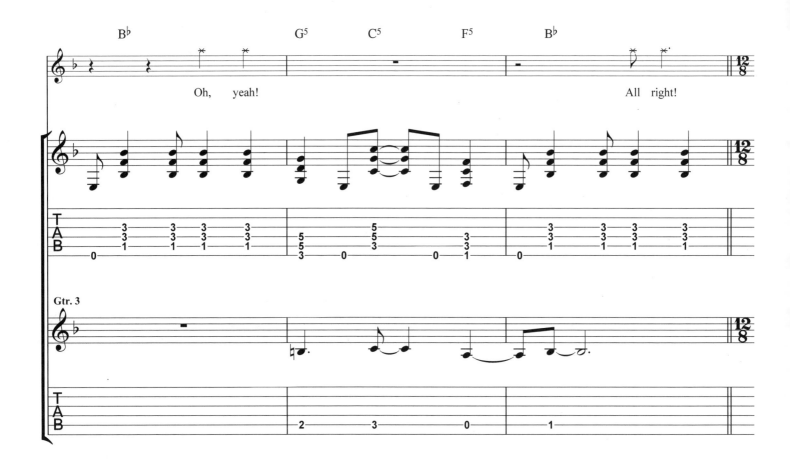

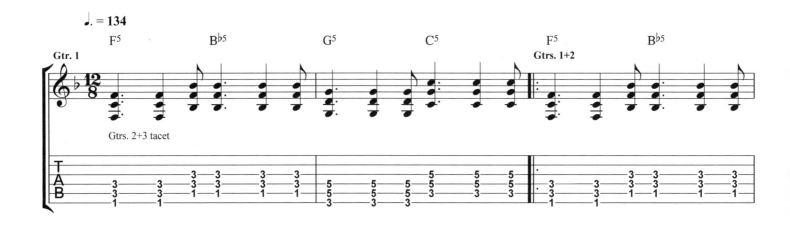

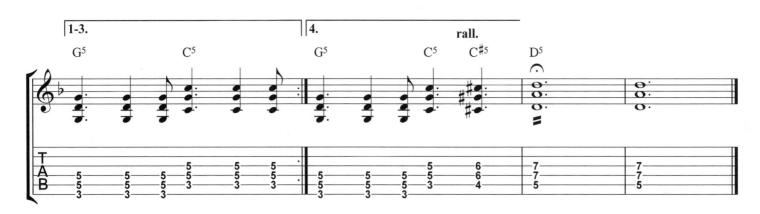

ATTENTION

WORDS & MUSIC BY
JACK WHITE & BRENDAN BENSON

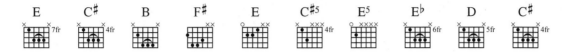

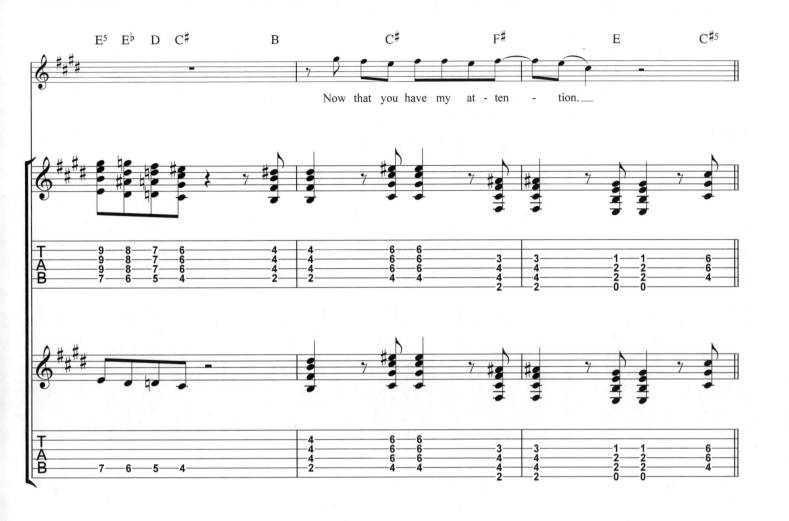

Now that you have my at - ten - tion.___

Interlude

Gtr. 2 tacet

67

Got some___ kind of vice___ like grip___ on___ me.___

Fig. 5

(C#)

1.

Gtr. 1 plays Fig. 5

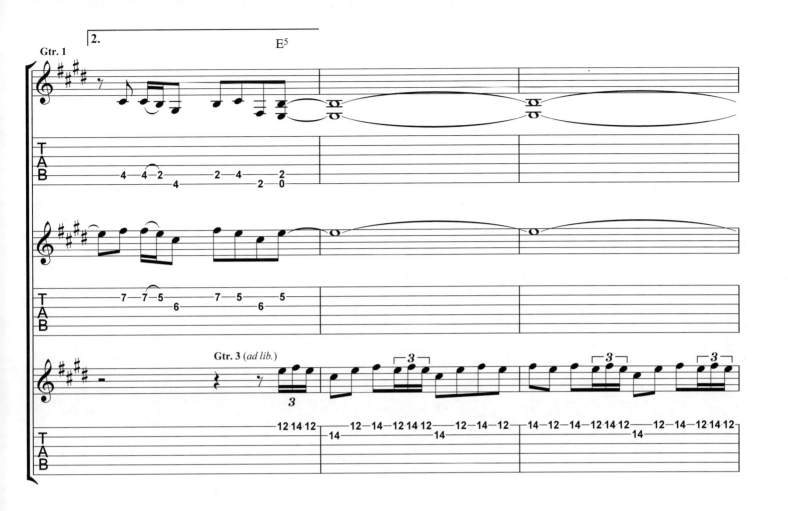

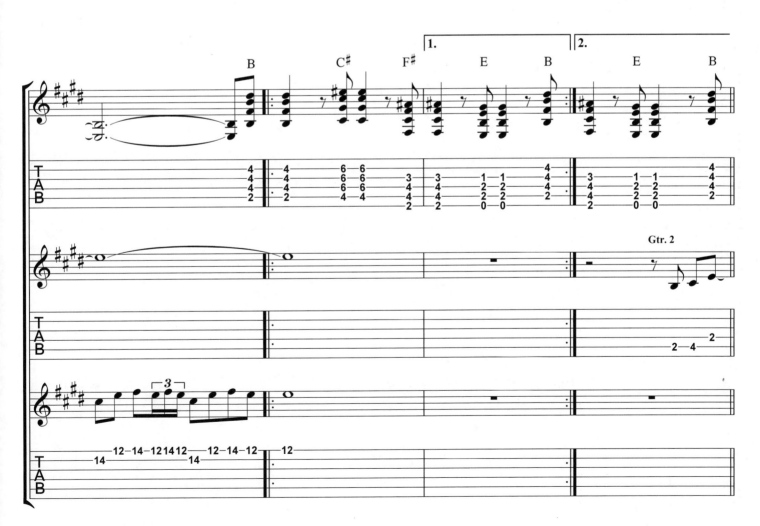

PULL THIS BLANKET OFF

WORDS & MUSIC BY
JACK WHITE & BRENDAN BENSON

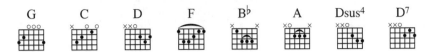

Verse

1. Pull this blan-ket off of me,___ may-be it -'ll help me see___
2. It's hard stick-ing to your guns___ when ev'-ry-bo-dy's hav-ing fun,___

the things I be-lieve___ to be true.___
makes me wan-na run, I don't know what to do.___

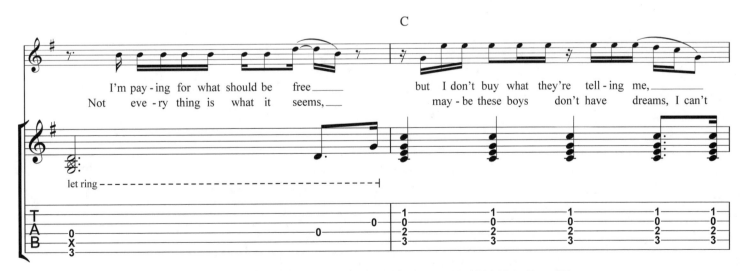

I'm pay-ing for what should be free___ but I don't buy what they're tell-ing me,___
Not ev-e-ry thing is what it seems,___ may-be these boys don't have dreams, I can't

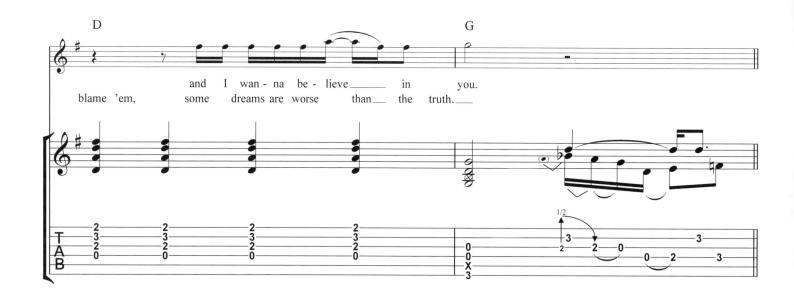

and I wan - na be - lieve_____ in you.
blame 'em, some dreams are worse than___ the truth.___

Interlude

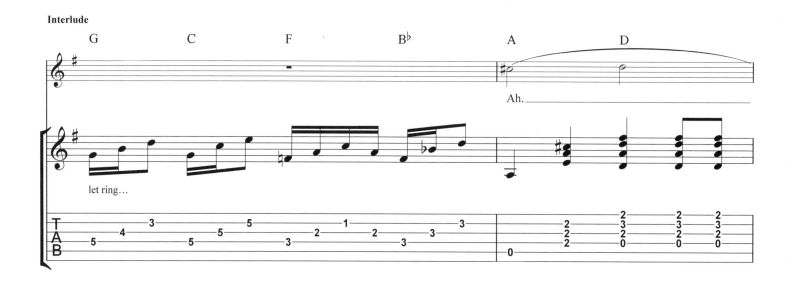

Ah.___

let ring…

Ah.___

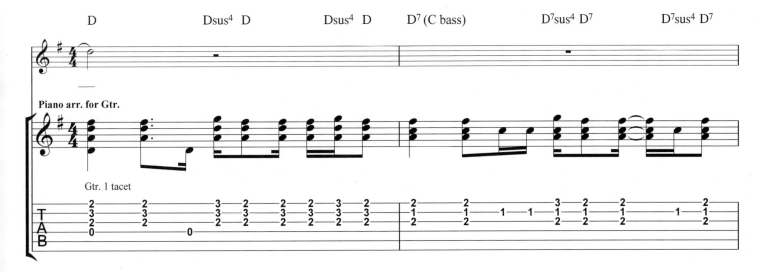

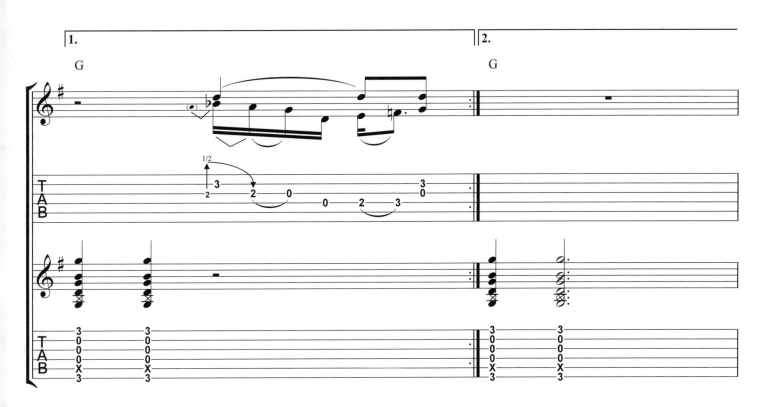

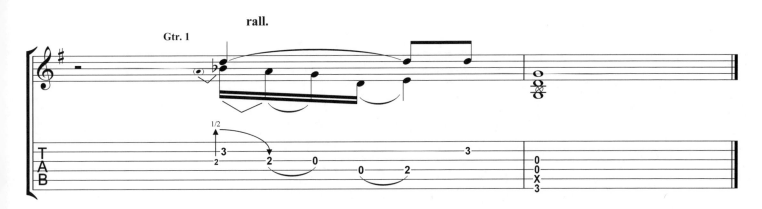

RICH KID BLUES

WORDS & MUSIC BY
TERENCE JAMES REID

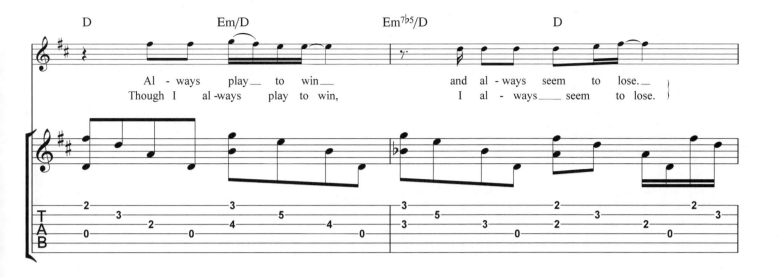

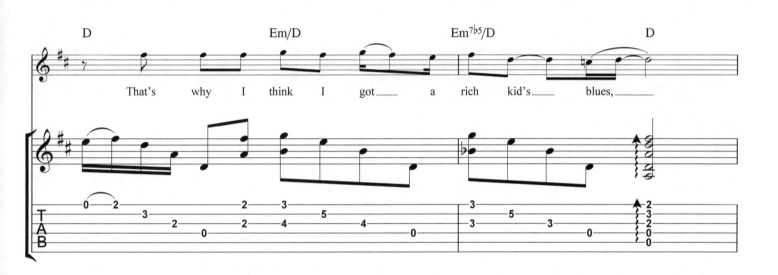

To Coda ⊕

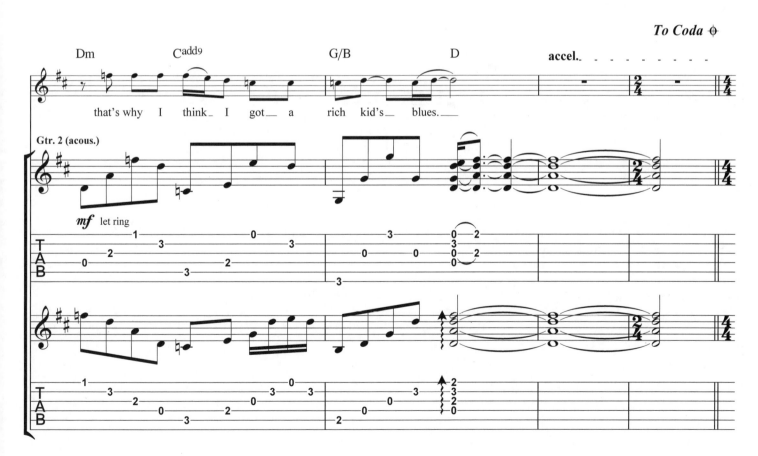

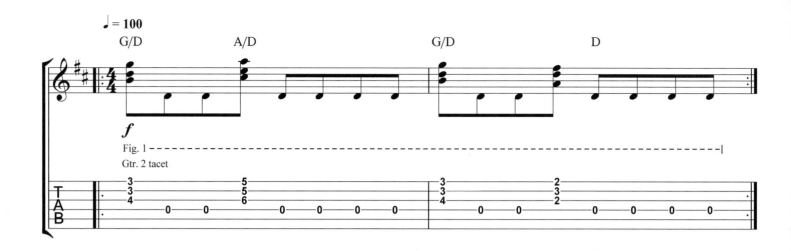

Chorus

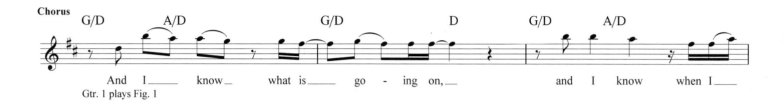

And I ___ know ___ what is ___ go - ing on, ___ and I know when I ___

Gtr. 1 plays Fig. 1

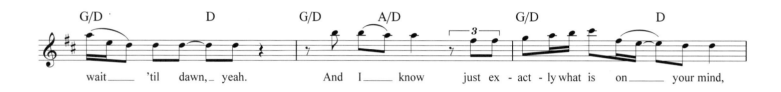

wait ___ 'til dawn, _ yeah. And I ___ know just ex - act - ly what is on ___ your mind,

But you'll be back, ___ I know it, but I'm still gon - na lose ___ you, ___ yeah.

N.C.

But I'm won - der - ing why, girl, did I ask ___ your name? And all the peo - ple stand - ing by ___ are

Gtr. 1 tacet

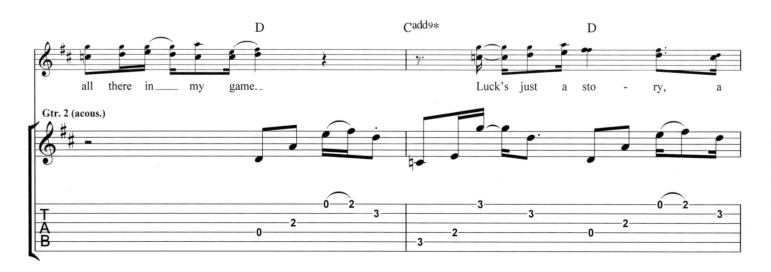

all there in ___ my game. _ Luck's just a sto - ry, a

Gtr. 2 (acous.)

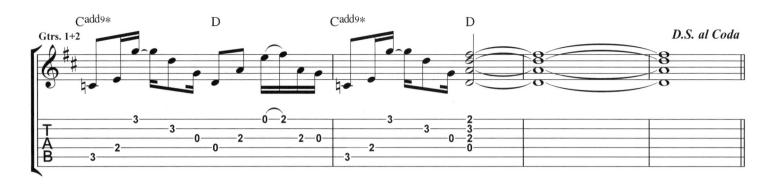

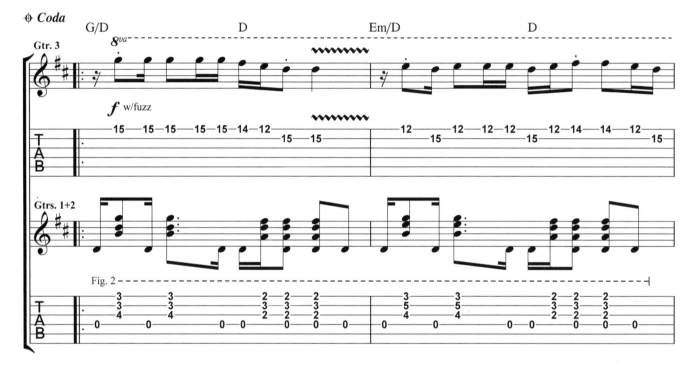

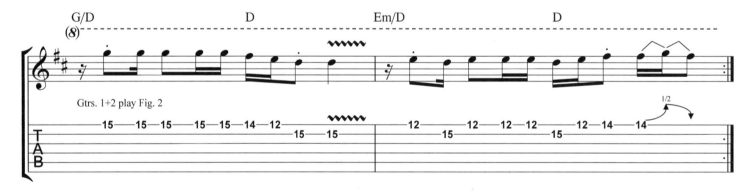

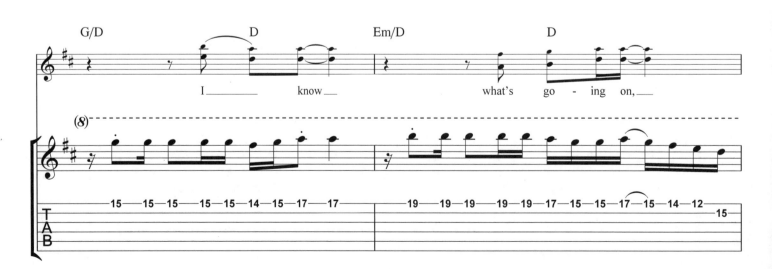

I_____ know___   what's go - ing on,___

THESE STONES WILL SHOUT

WORDS & MUSIC BY
JACK WHITE & BRENDAN BENSON

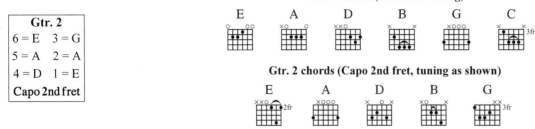

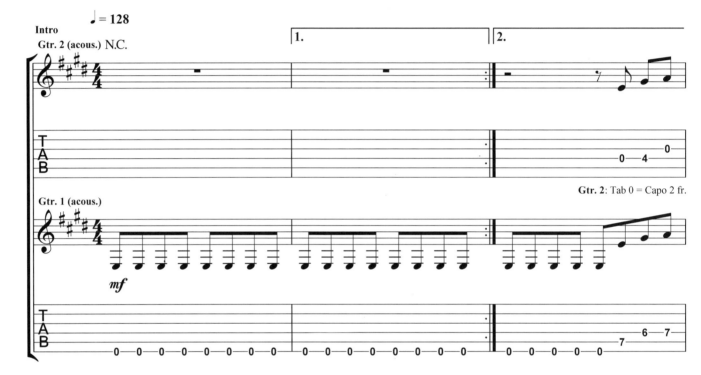

Verse

pressed me so __ com - plete - ly, I start ob - ses - sing to hear __ from you. __ What ev - er

Gtr. 1 w/ Fig. 1
Gtr. 2 w/ Fig. 2

you do, you __ do sweet - ly, it takes a lot to not take __ from __ you. __

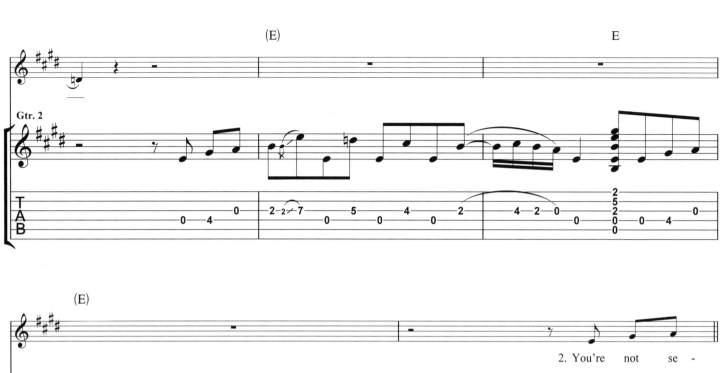

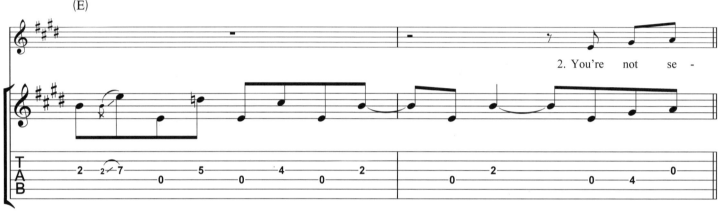

Verse

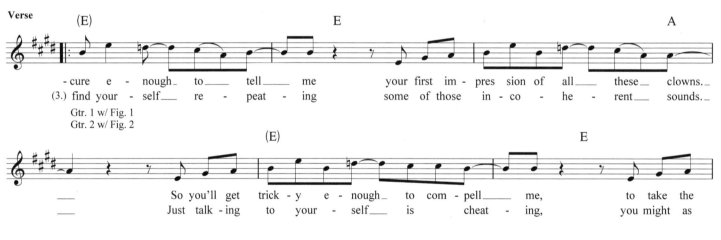

-cure e - nough___ to___ tell___ me your first im - pres sion of all___ these___ clowns.___
(3.) find your - self___ re - peat - ing some of those in - co - he - rent___ sounds.___

Gtr. 1 w/ Fig. 1
Gtr. 2 w/ Fig. 2

___ So you'll get trick - y e - nough___ to com - pell___ me, to take the
___ Just talk - ing to your - self___ is cheat - ing, you might as

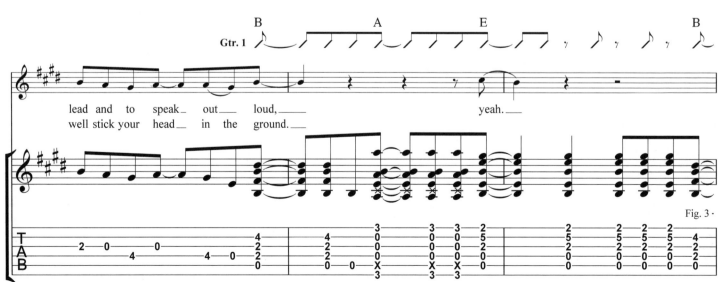

lead and to speak out___ loud,___ yeah.___
well stick your head___ in the ground.___

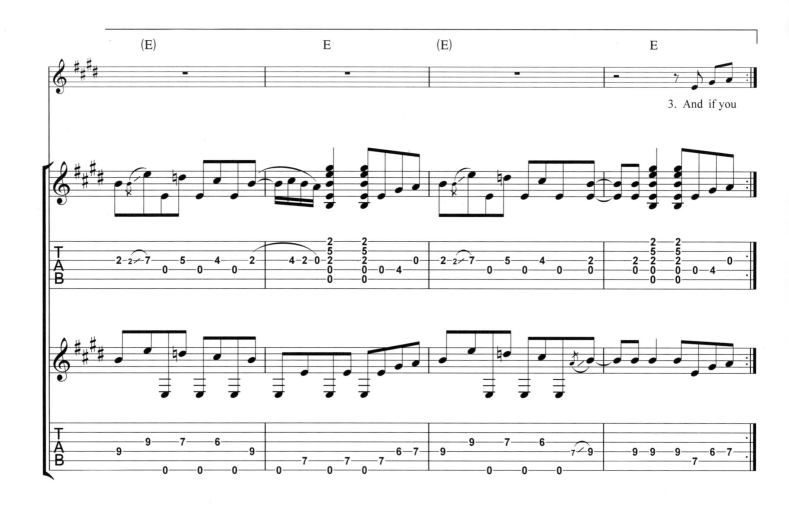

3. And if you

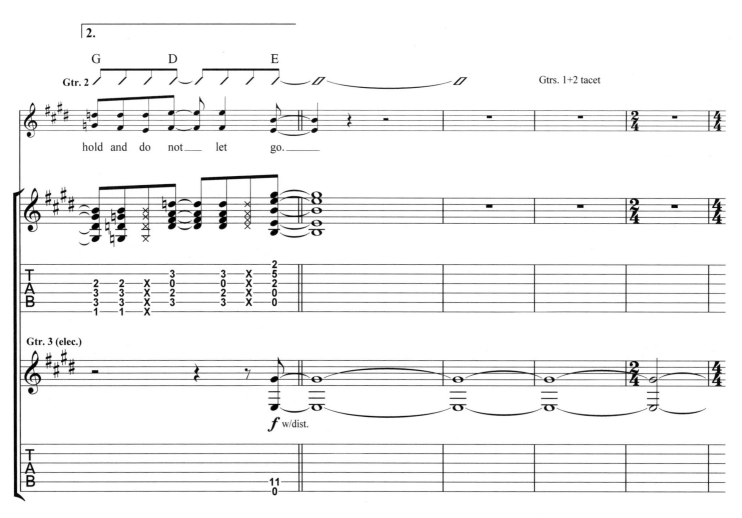

hold and do not____ let go.____

Bridge

I feel com - pelled to just yell   out for you,

to say   the words that you can't bring out. ___   But I   can - not do ev'-ry - thing for you

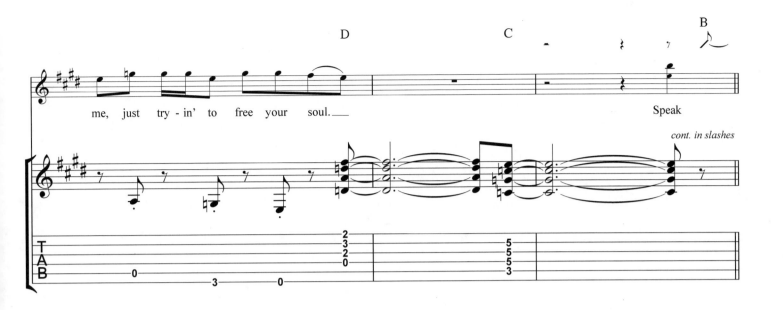

me, just try-in' to free your soul.___ Speak

cont. in slashes

Chorus

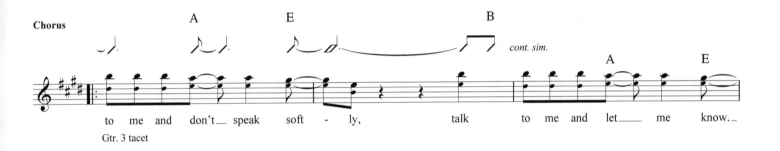

to me and don't___ speak soft - ly, talk to me and let___ me know.___

Gtr. 3 tacet

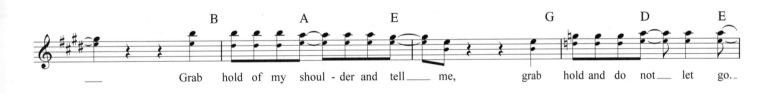

___ Grab hold of my shoul - der and tell___ me, grab hold and do not___ let go.___

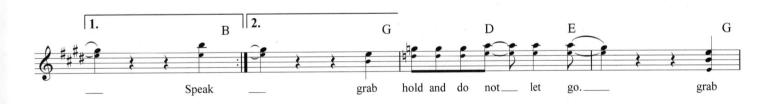

1. ___ Speak **2.** ___ grab hold and do not___ let go.___ grab

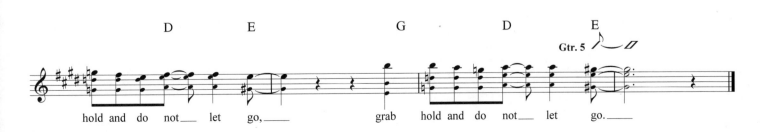

hold and do not___ let go,___ grab hold and do not___ let go.___

CAROLINA DRAMA

WORDS & MUSIC BY
JACK WHITE & BRENDAN BENSON

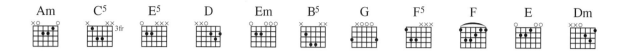

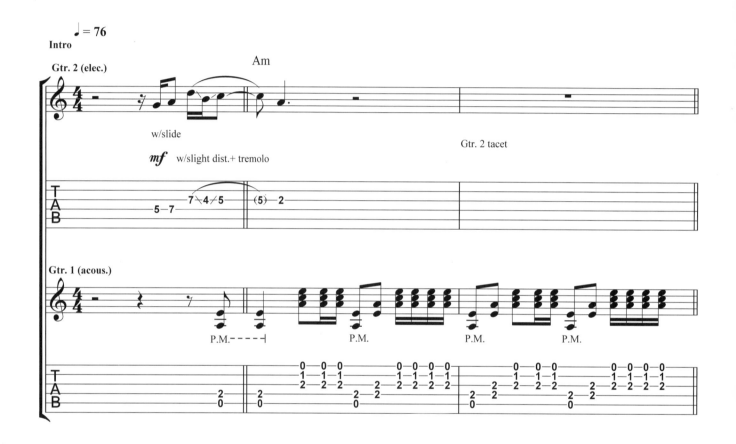

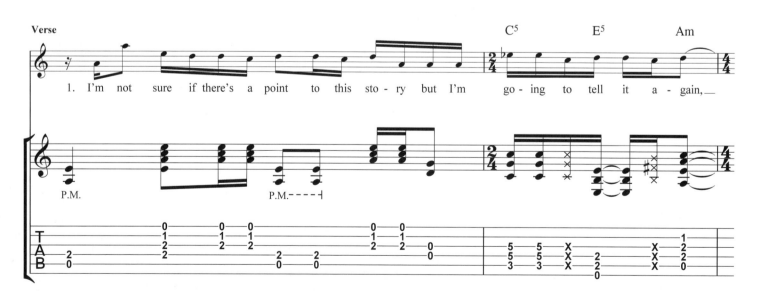

1. I'm not sure if there's a point to this sto-ry but I'm go-ing to tell it a-gain,

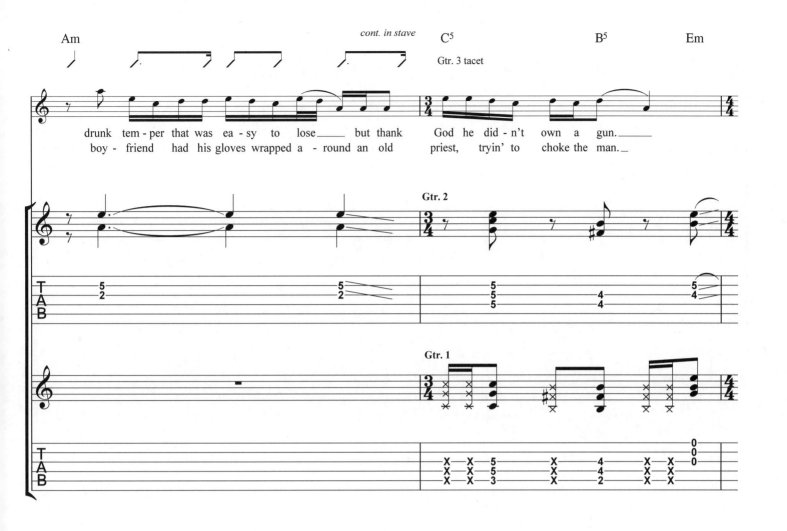

drunk tem - per that was ea - sy to lose_____ but thank God he did - n't own a gun._____
boy - friend had his gloves wrapped a - round an old priest, tryin' to choke the man._

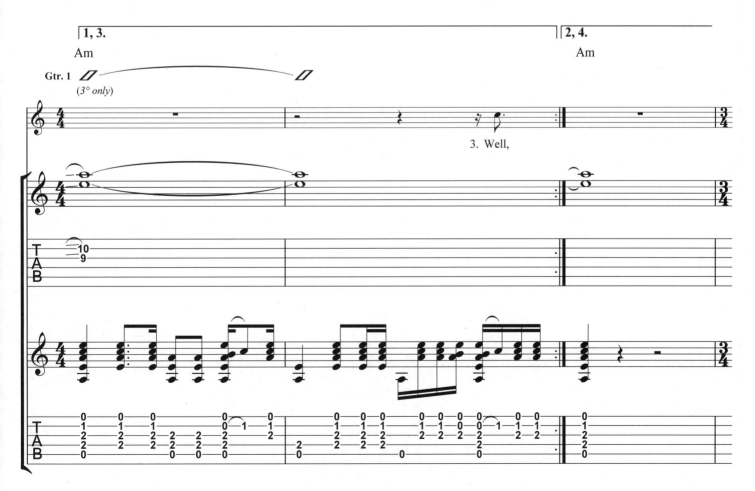

3. Well,

Interlude

1.

ah. _____ ah, _____ ah. _____

let ring… cont. *ad lib.*

cont. in slashes

2.

Verse

Am

Gtr. 1   cont. sim.

6. Bil - ly broke in and saw the blood on the floor __ and   he turned a - round and put the lock on the door, __
(Verses 7–8 see block lyrics)

Dm   E

he looked dead in - to the boy - friend's eye, __   his moth - er was a ghost, too up - set to cry. __ well,

Am

he took a step t'ward the man on the ground, _ from his mouth trick-led out a lit-tle au-di-ble sound. _

Dm   **E**   *Play 3 times*

He heard the boy-friend shout, "Get out!" _ and Bil-ly said, "Not till I know what this is all a - bout."

Am

La - la, la - la, la - la, la - la,_____ yeah. La - la, la - la, la - la, la - la,_____ yeah.

Dm   **E**

La - la, la - la, la - la, la - la,_____ yeah. la, la - la,____ la, la - la. _____

rit.

F   **E**   *cont. in stave*

La - la, la - la, la - la, la - la,____ yeah, _ La - la, la - la, la - la, la - la,____ yeah, _

Am

La - la, la - la, la - la, la - la,____ yeah, _ La - la, la - la, la - la, la - la,____ yeah, _

Gtr. 1

Verse 4:
Billy looked up from the window to the truck
Threw up, and had to struggle to stand
He saw that red-necked bastard with a hammer
Turn the priest into a shell of a man
The priest was putting up the fight of his life
But he was old and he was bound to lose
The boyfriend hit as hard as he could
And knocked the priest right down to his shoes.

Verse 5:
Well, now Billy knew but never actually met
The preacher lying there in the room
He heard himself say, "That must be my daddy"
Then he knew what he was gonna do
Billy got up enough courage
To get up and grabbed the first blunt thing he could find
It was a cold, glass bottle of milk
That got delivered every morning at nine.

Verse 7:
"Well, this preacher here was attacking your mama"
But Billy knew this, he was caught in a drama
So Billy took dead aim at his face
And smashed the bottle on the man who left his Dad in disgrace
And the white milk dripped down with the blood
And the boyfriend fell down dead for good
Right next to the preacher who was gasping for air
And Billy shouted, "Daddy, why d'ya have to come back here?"

Verse 8:
His mama reached behind the sugar and honey
And pulled out an envelope filled with money
"Your daddy gave us this," she collapsed in tears
"He's been paying all the bills for years"
"Mama, let's put this body underneath the trees,
And put Daddy in the truck and head to Tennessee"
Just then, his little brother came in
Holding the milkman's hat and a bottle of gin singing.

GUITAR TABLATURE EXPLAINED

Guitar music can be notated in three different ways: on a musical stave, in tablature, and in rhythm slashes.

RHYTHM SLASHES: are written above the stave. Strum chords in the rhythm indicated. Round noteheads indicate single notes.

THE MUSICAL STAVE: shows pitches and rhythms and is divided by lines into bars. Pitches are named after the first seven letters of the alphabet.

TABLATURE: graphically represents the guitar fingerboard. Each horizontal line represents a string, and each number represents a fret.

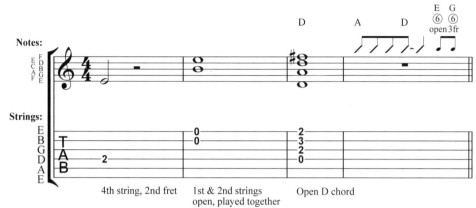

4th string, 2nd fret   1st & 2nd strings open, played together   Open D chord

Definitions for special guitar notation

SEMI-TONE BEND: Strike the note and bend up a semi-tone (½ step).

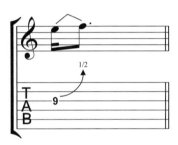

BEND & RELEASE: Strike the note and bend up as indicated, then release back to the original note.

HAMMER-ON: Strike the first note with one finger, then sound the second note (on the same string) with another finger by fretting it without picking.

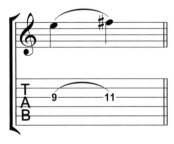

NATURAL HARMONIC: Strike the note while the fret-hand lightly touches the string directly over the fret indicated.

WHOLE-TONE BEND: Strike the note and bend up a whole-tone (full step).

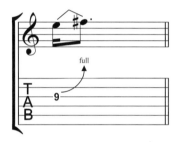

COMPOUND BEND & RELEASE: Strike the note and bend up and down in the rhythm indicated.

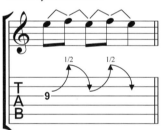

PULL-OFF: Place both fingers on the note to be sounded, strike the first note and without picking, pull the finger off to sound the second note.

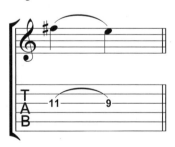

PICK SCRAPE: The edge of the pick is rubbed down (or up) the string, producing a scratchy sound.

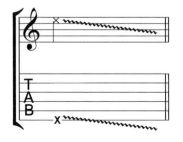

GRACE NOTE BEND: Strike the note and bend as indicated. Play the first note as quickly as possible.

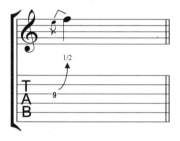

PRE-BEND: Bend the note as indicated, then strike it.

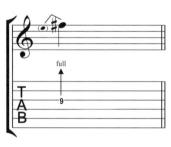

LEGATO SLIDE (GLISS): Strike the first note and then slide the same fret-hand finger up or down to the second note. The second note is not struck.

PALM MUTING: The note is partially muted by the pick hand lightly touching the string(s) just before the bridge.

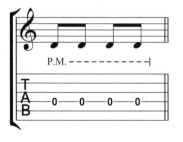

QUARTER-TONE BEND: Strike the note and bend up a ¼ step

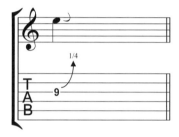

PRE-BEND & RELEASE: Bend the note as indicated. Strike it and release the note back to the original pitch.

MUFFLED STRINGS: A percussive sound is produced by laying the first hand across the string(s) without depressing, and striking them with the pick hand.

SHIFT SLIDE (GLISS & RESTRIKE) Same as legato slide, except the second note is struck.

1 2 3 4 5 6 7 8 9